Traveling the Road to..

Dr. Mia Y. Merritt

Copyright © 2014
by
Mia Y. Merritt, Ph.D
Traveling the Road to Success

All rights reserved. No part of this publication may be reproduced, distributed, or transmitted in any form or by any means, including photocopying, recording, or other electronic or mechanical methods, without the prior written permission of the author or publisher, except in the case of brief quotations embodied in critical reviews and certain other noncommercial uses permitted by copyright law.

ISBN # 9781628900941

Other Books by Mia Y. Merritt:
The Cost of the Anointing
The Cost of the Anointing Workbook
Releasing Emotional Baggage
Prosperity is Your Birthright!
Prosperity is Your Birthright Workbook
Destined for Great Things!
Destined for Great Things Workbook
Words of Inspiration: Golden Nuggets for the Wise at Heart
Life After High School
Life After High School Workbook
All About the Military
Money and how it Multiplies
Money and how it Multiplies Workbook
Traveling The Road to Success
The Road to Inner Joy

Library of Congress Cataloging
in-Publication Data

Merritt, Mia

First Printing 2014
Printed in the U.S.A.

Introduction

The position of sustainable success is open and available for everyone to apply. No prior experience is needed, but you must be willing to put in long hours, work late, sometimes on weekends, and be willing to travel if necessary. You set your own schedule and decide your own salary. You will be paid according to the effort you put in. However, as you continue to diligently work hard, your wages will double because the seeds you plant will multiply. There is no deadline to apply, but the sooner you are ready to work, the sooner you get the job!

Massive success is attainable for anyone living in the United States with a reasonable degree of health and strength, but the elevator to success is broken. You must take the stairs. Taking the stairs means that the journey will not be an easy ride. It is going to take some toil, sweat, labor, tears, sleepless nights, and getting tired along the way; but as you persevere, you will find that you will see the top stair and will make it. The only place where success comes before work is in the dictionary. There is no meaningful achievement without labor and work. The successful life is a disciplined life! Most people live in mediocrity or slightly above or below it because they are too mentally lazy to put forth the self-discipline necessary to find the road out of lack and limitation and travel it. This book delineates practical, yet powerful success principles that when applied, will take you to great heights of achievement. Successful people do the things that average people do not like to do. The successful are strategic with their time, wise in their decisions, prudent in their judgment, and they plan their work and work their plan. Welcome to success!

Dedication

This book is dedicated to my only son and five nephews: Stephan Sanders (15); Landon Ivory (10); Dylan Ivory (4); Karrieem Nasai (KJ) (15); Christopher Espey (11) and Amari Freeman (11).

As African American young men, you must go over and beyond the average boy your age to prove yourself in this world. Each of you has your own unique gifts, abilities, and skills. It is my prayer that you will cultivate and nurture the gifts that are inside you until they take you to great heights of accomplishment and success. You were not created to linger in the background, nor were you created to be mediocre. You were created to make a significant contribution to the world through *your* skills, *your* gifts, *your* talents, and *your* abilities. The greatness inside of you will not be known to the world until you begin to work in a spirit of excellence. Self-discipline will take you to greatness. Honesty and integrity will earn you respect and loyal friends. Hard work will earn you success. Humility will earn you favor. As soon-to-be adult men, I encourage you to rise to the top through hard work, toil, sacrifice, and self-discipline. Make your mark in this world and let nothing stop you from being the men that God called you and created to be.

Love,
Mommy/Auntie Mia

Praise Reports for
Traveling the Road to Success

Dr. Merritt never ceases to amaze me with her writings. After reading this powerful book, I saw myself in many of the principles that she described. I am proud to say that I actually do implement several of them in my profession, but I did see a couple that I need to work on. I recommend this book to be read by professionals and leaders from all backgrounds. It will definitely propel them to the next level of success!

Barbara Watson, State Representative
Florida District #107

Dr. Merritt's book gives practical, everyday strategies for reaching success. Her simplistic, yet profound principles will work in the life of the determined, if you work them. This book is a must read for people from all walks of life!

Dr. Jaffus Hardrick, Vice President
Florida International University
Division of Human Resources

We have always heard that if there is no pain, there is no gain. Dr. Merritt has eloquently and profoundly delineated in her book, how gain emerges through hard work and toil. However, I love where she expounds upon how embracing a positive attitude has a direct connection to success. It is my opinion that everyone desiring to be elevated to another level personally and business-wise read the principles outlined in 'Traveling The Road to Success'!

Dr. Wilbert Holloway, School Board Member
Miami-Dade County Public Schools District #1

'Traveling The Road to Success' is a must read! As a business person myself, I was able to see many of the principles that are definite keys to success, but I was also able to gain a new level of insight on some principles that I will be applying to take my life and business to another level.

Lakitsia Gaines, President
Lakitsia Gaines Insurance Agency Inc.

After reading 'Prosperity is Your Birthright', I did not think she could top that, but I must say as a student of success principles, I recommend this book to be read by students, entrepreneurs, professionals, housewives, and individuals from all backgrounds. 'Traveling The Road to Success' is an easy and practical read, but the teachings are profoundly powerful and will definitely take the reader to a new level of thought.

Ann McNeill, Founder
International Mastermind Association
President, MCO Construction & Services

After reading this book, I felt as though I needed to be doing so much more. As a pastor, I teach service, work, faith, and love, but I also teach that faith without works is dead. Dr. Merritt's book not only expounds upon the importance of hard work, but outlines how to strategically perform and get benefits in return. I will be recommending this book to everyone that I know.

Dwayne Richardson, Pastor
Greater Love Full Gospel Baptist Church

I was so intrigued by this book that I began practicing some of the new principles immediately. I could see the practicality in each principle, and realized that they only took a degree of self-discipline to apply. For the person who desires to take their lives to the next level, this book is a must read.

Dr. Venessa Walker, Chiropractic Physician
Health Wellness Speaker

After reading Dr. Merritt's Book, 'Traveling The Road to Success' all I could say is, wow! What a practical, information-filled, and profoundly applicable piece of literature that will benefit any and everyone interested in achieving success. Thank you Dr. Merritt, for this powerful piece of literature!

Dr. John Fontaine
Fountaine & Fountaine Corp/Government/Institutional
HR Consultants

I am so proud of Dr. Merritt and her accomplishments. As her spiritual mentor and friend, I find her to be a woman of integrity, great faith, and diligence. The wisdom that God has imparted into her is remarkable. I pray that God's favor continues to rein in her life as she stays in His will and continues on the path leading to the kingdom of God.

Dr. Dennis M. Jackson, Pastor
United Christian Praise and Worship Center

Table of Contents

Chapter 1: Set Your Mind 1

Chapter 2: Overcoming Obstacles 13

Chapter 3: Self & Self-Discipline 31

Chapter 4: Strategic Goal-setting 47

Chapter 5: The Foundation of Success 63

Chapter 6: Inner Healing 85

Chapter 7: From Good to Great 97

Chapter 8: Can you Handle Success? 107

Chapter 9: Giving Back 123

About the Author 135

Discussion Questions for Book clubs 136

Other Books by Dr. Mia Y. Merritt 137

Recommended Readings 138

Traveling the...
Road to Success

Dr. Mia Y. Merritt

1
Set Your Mind!

If your mind can conceive it and your heart can believe it, then you can achieve it! ~Author unknown

When it comes to success, everyone has different definitions because it means different things to different people. When people use phrases such as, *He is a successful businessman; She has had much success in her field; I've not had much success in selling,* they are usually referring to money-making because people equate money with success, but having money and being successful do not always go hand-in-hand. Most often it does, but not always. Some people are successful, but have very low bank accounts; others have lots of money, but are still failures in life. How is that? Because the view of success is different to different people. The bottom line is that success is not always measured in dollars and cents. It is definitely measured in commonsense, but not always dollars and cents. Believe it or not, not everyone wants lots of money. Not everyone desires a big home, an expensive car, and sophisticated toys. Not having those things does not mean that a person is not successful. They may very well be successful in their own right without possessing "things." In order to be considered a success, one must do all they endeavor to do in a spirit of excellence and have total peace about it. After all, if you are productive in the s mall things that you are given to do, then you will eventually graduate to greater things with greater responsibility. The secret of success is to do the common things uncommonly well. No one will entrust you with greater responsibility until you become known for being faithful over small things. Therefore, you must begin to do small things in a great way. It does not matter how small the task, do it well. No one can doubt your greatness if you show it in your actions. In all your relations, be great. This is considered success because you have demonstrated and applied the principle and character of success in all that you do.

Money often comes as a byproduct of doing things with excellence. When seeking to arrive at a level of success that will gravitate money to you, there are certain principles that must be applied, and the most basic of them is to set your mind in a success mode and keep it there. When you are determined to succeed, then nothing, no one, no situation, circumstance, or obstacle should be able to move your mind out of the success position that it has been set. Your mind is the most powerful asset you have because it controls everything you do. Your mind controls what you say, where you go, what you wear, how you treat people, what you buy, and it even controls the condition of your physical body. It is time that we understand just how powerful the mind is because once we learn to control the mind, we will ultimately control our own destinies. Most people have heard the saying, *The mind is a terrible thing to waste.* Oh, how true that is! When you do not deliberately monitor the position of your mind, it will wander to and fro, here and there, and feed upon whatever reaches it as the result of your neglect. Successful people have an unwavering focus on whatever it is they aspire to do, and their unmitigated gall to be successful does not allow their minds to divert from their objective. The ultimate mastery of the human mind is when one entertains only thoughts that are positive, constructive, creative, peaceful and fruit-bearing. Great people have great thoughts. You cannot have a positive life and a negative mind. If you have a negative mind, you will have a negative life. You are changing every day, and as your mind changes for the better, your life changes for the better. Thoughts bear fruit and when your thoughts are good, the fruit of your life is good. You can look at a person's attitude and immediately know the nature of thoughts they most often think. Thousands of thoughts enter the mind everyday; therefore, we must be constantly filtering thoughts 24 hours a day. No thought should be able to reside in your mind for long if it is not of a positive nature. You must always guard your thoughts well because what you think in your secret thoughts today (good or bad), will manifest into your life tomorrow.

    We all are where we are because of where our thoughts have brought us, and we will be in the future where our thoughts take us. Our character today is the culmination of our thoughts of the past. Your life is what you have made it by your thoughts. Once you get full control of your mind, you will have full control of your life. You have no personality and no life apart from your thoughts. They are always right where you are. They are never separated from you. As your thoughts change, you will change also. Success will not come as a result of wishing for it long enough; nor will it come by repeating positive affirmations each day or praying hard for it without doing anything else. Success will come the old fashion way - hard work. The aforementioned actions will significantly help, but only when hard work is the foundation upon which all other things are built will they help. Once you have it in your mind that you will become and remain successful no matter what, that you will not allow your mind to move from the positive position it has been set, and that you will work hard in the areas that will bring you success, then there is no way that you should not acquire the success that you are endeavoring to achieve! Life returns back to you what you put in it.

Thoughts are Things

Everything you are, everything you do, everywhere you go, the decisions you make, the job that you have, and even the clothes that you wear first originated in your mind. What you see in the material form had two births. First, there was the mental birth where the thought was conceived. Then, there was the physical birth when the thoughts materialized. For example, if your mind tells you that you are hungry and are craving pizza, that is the first birth. You then begin to desire pizza so much that you can taste it. After the pizza is delivered or after you go and pick it up, your thought has then become the thing. Thoughts are things. The thought was pulled out of the mental realm and brought into the natural realm. The book that you are reading right now was first a thought. In my mind was where the first birth originated. I pulled the thought out of my mind by writing my concept for the book. I then developed outlines and organized chapters. I watered the thought by writing daily and making covers for the book. The book in your hand is the second birth. The first birth was the seed. The second birth is the harvest. Everything has two births.

If we know that thoughts are things, then why should we not begin to strategically conceive thoughts and purposefully allow them to become things? Recognize the thoughts that are worthy of attention because some are not worth entertaining and must be dismissed. Some thoughts that come to us are fruitless and foolish. I still get outlandish and foolish thoughts that come to me and when I recognize them, I say to myself, *"Where in the world did that come from?"* Then, I simply release it. Other thoughts can be negative and destructive. They too must be dismissed. Just because you receive such thoughts does not mean that you are a bad person. Everyone receives negative thoughts - everyone! But it is the wise person who can recognize the bad thoughts and eradicate them. We constantly pick up the thoughts of others from their vibrations. Sometimes thoughts come to our minds and we think they belong to us when they really have come from others. These thoughts linger in the invisible realm looking for an outlet of expression. When you release them from your mind, they continue to linger until another mind picks them up and acts on them. The key is to recognize those that will bear no positive fruit and evict them immediately! When negative, dishonest, sinister thoughts enter your mind and you entertain them, they feel comfortable coming back, so they return. As you continue to entertain them a second and a third time, they begin seeking an outlet of expression through you. Thoughts are things, so as soon as an opportunity to materialize appears, the negative thought becomes a thing. Those negative, deceitful, sinister thoughts manifest and become a cause. After you have initiated the cause, you must be prepared for the effect that will result. Thoughts are seeds, and when planted in the mind, then cultivated and watered, will bring forth a harvest. The harvest will either be good or bad. It is up to you and is based upon the nature of the seed sown. Other thoughts are of a positive nature, such as when it inspires you to do something nice for someone for no particular reason. Sometimes your mind tells you to call a certain person just to see how they are doing. Those thoughts are good seeds and will return a good harvest. Where there is a cause, there will also be an effect. Other thoughts are actual ideas that come out of the mind of the

Creator and are then released into the earth realm to human minds. The mind that picks up the idea should not only entertain it momentarily then forget about it, but that mind must cultivate and nurture the idea until it materializes. When steps are taken for the manifestation of the idea to occur, that person will get the reward.

Thinking negatively has more detrimental effects than you know. What we think is actually reflected in our facial expressions. Your attitude is your inward thinking expressed by outward behavior. You cannot be thinking negative thoughts and have a beautiful smile on your face. You cannot be thinking beautiful thoughts and have a frown on your face. Your mind is like a computer - junk in, junk out. Your thoughts, emotions, and facial expressions go hand-in-hand; but more important than that is the fact that when you entertain negative, disappointing, or evil thoughts, your body begins to weaken. It sinks into a position that causes sickness and disease. At the command of pleasant, beautiful, and noble thoughts, the body becomes clothed with youthfulness and beauty. Strong, pure, and positive thinking build up the body in health, strength, and grace. Out of a clean heart, comes clean thoughts and a clean life. To renew your body, you must beautify your mind with positive thinking. Negative thoughts of unforgiveness, hatred, guilt, shame, and bitterness rob the body of its vitality and health. Clean thoughts also make clean habits. You must monitor your thinking in order to be truly successful. Your attitude will also affect your courage to pursue a worthy goal. If you are doubtful or fearful, you will not even try to go after something you inwardly desire. King David was a perfect example of how a fearless attitude can bring forth courage. When it came to killing a Philistine giant who was constantly mocking, intimidating, and embarrassing the Israelites, forty-thousand Israelite soldiers all thought, "Goliath is so big that we can never kill him." But David looked at the same giant and thought, "Goliath is so big that there is no way I can miss him." His attitude bred his courage!

The Mind & the Brain

All too often, these two words, brain and mind are used interchangeably but they are not synonymous terms. The brain is an organ, which is matter. It is a part of the central nervous system, which is continuous with the spinal cord. It includes all the higher nervous centers enclosed within the skull. The biggest part of the brain is the cerebrum, which makes up 85% of the brain's weight. The cerebrum is the thinking part of the brain and it controls voluntary muscles. When you are thinking very hard, you are using your cerebrum. Both your short-term and long-term memory lives there. The cerebrum has two halves, one on the left and one on the right side of the head. It has been determined that the right half causes us to think about abstract things such as music, colors, and shapes. The left half is said to be more analytical, helping with mathematics, logic, and speech. The left side is commonly used for thought and the retention of knowledge. Doctors have discovered that the right half of the cerebrum controls the left side of the body, and the left half controls the right side. An injury to the right half of the brain will cause some paralysis of a muscle on the left side and vice versa.

Understanding the relationship between the physical brain and the functional mind is not a difficult one. The first thing you should know is that the mind is not produced by the brain. The mind enhances the brain through thought instead of the brain making thought. The brain is merely the instrument of the one who thinks, just as a piano is the instrument of the one who plays. Just as a piano can do nothing by itself, the brain can do nothing without the mind. In a nutshell, the brain is only a recording instrument for the mind and personality behind it. When you were born, the record in your brain was blank. There was no impression made on any part as yet. No one knew what you were to become or grow into. You could have been a doctor, lawyer, teacher, politician, mechanic, vagabond, con-artist, or murderer. No one knew. It was all dependent upon the seed that was concealed within your mind, which would eventually shape your personality. Your environment played a vital role in what you evolved into as well as the experiences and exposures you had, but it was your mind that determined how your environment was going to affect you. There were already certain genetic tendencies in your make-up inherited from your ancestors, but those are easy to overcome by placing opposing habits in place of the unfavorable ones. You can imprint whatever you want upon your brain, but it is your *mind* that determines how you will respond to those things. The brain is like a tape recorder which records things on a particular locality and then retrieves them upon request. Brain-building requires mental labor, concentration and self-discipline, but the reward is great for the person who makes the sacrifice. If your mind develops in you, the desire for a noble personality, you will imprint upon your brain the desire for this noble change. You cannot show forth an honest, noble, and amiable personality until your mind gives you the desire for it. The brain can never do opposite of what the mind gives it. It is commonly understood that the consistent use of certain faculties is dependent upon certain localities in the brain. There is a locality for speaking, reading, computing mathematical figures, singing, dancing, and playing musical instruments. According to the tools you give it, so will the expression of your soul be. Desires originate in the mind first, then are written upon the brain. The mental or physical exercise needed is then executed. What really matters is the desire in your mind to progress in positive ways. That is what makes your personality. The mind simply makes the expression through the brain. We often make two mistakes as it pertains to brainpower. We underestimate our own and overestimate the brain-power of others. The people that we perceive as highly intelligent are only those who have exercised the self-discipline that it takes to enhance their mind, but it is not brainpower that we should seek. It is actually "mind" power. The thing to do is to stop seeking to become smarter through brain-building, but actually strive to become wiser through mind development.

> *The mind is a powerful tool, but as with any tool, we must learn to properly use it. The mind can be a great servant but a horrible master!*

Master Your Mind

Now that we have a clear understanding of how powerful the mind is and how we can filter negative thoughts out of it, and cultivate positive thoughts to become things, we need to now take the necessary steps to master the mind. Unless we learn to be the master of our minds, we will never find the fulfillment, contentment, and peace that we inwardly desire. The mind is a powerful tool, but as with any tool, we must learn to properly use it. The mind can be a great servant but a horrible master! We should be the master of our minds and not the servant to it. With proper discipline, everyone can control and master their minds. There is a law of mind that dictates that whatever you pay attention to is what you become conscious of. Begin to pay attention to the thoughts that enter your mind. If you don't, then you will never be able to master it. As you begin to monitor your thoughts, you will begin to see both the positive and negative tendencies. Your life is determined by the quality of thoughts you have and how you act upon those thoughts. Those who are not conscious of their thoughts will feed off of whatever reaches it from the environment. Research has shown that the average person has between 50,000-70,000 thoughts that run through the mind daily and that about 85% of those thoughts are from the day before. This means that how we think is a function of habit and conditioning.

    Your character is the culmination of your thoughts. As your thoughts are modified, you change. You have become what you already are, but you are still becoming what you will be by your thoughts. You and only you, can change your character and your life simply by changing your thoughts. Life is operated by the law of cause and effect. The causes originate in the mind. If you lie, you will be lied to; if you cheat, you will be cheated; if you give hate, you will be hated by someone; if you give love, you will be loved by others, If you give criticism, you will be criticized. Wherever there is an effect, there is always a corresponding cause. To change the effect, we must change the cause, and if we trace the cause back far enough, we will discover that it can be found in the mental attitude which created the thought. Thoughts acted upon become causes. Causes bring effects. Effects then become new causes and those causes turn into effects, which then become causes, etc. It is therefore important how we react to effects. Success is contingent upon the way we think. To live is to think and act, and to think and act is to change. Everyone everywhere thinks and acts every day. If you are not thinking and acting, then you are not living. You are only existing. Even if you are ignorant of this fact, you are still changing for better or worse. We can become masters of ourselves because we have the power to control our thoughts. We must get ourselves right by monitoring our way of thinking. Weak are they who allow their thoughts to control their actions; strong are they who force their actions to control their thoughts. Take charge of your thoughts. Let your mind feast upon the things that will bring you peace, joy, happiness, love, prosperity, success and abundance. You have the power to master your mind.

Success Keys

* The ultimate mastery of the human mind is when one entertains only thoughts that are positive, constructive, creative, peaceful and fruit-bearing. You cannot have a positive life and a negative mind.

* All matter has two births. First, there is the mental birth of where the thought is conceived. The first birth is the seed. Then there is the physical birth of when the thoughts are materialized.

* Your mind is the most powerful asset you have because it controls everything you do. Your mind controls what you say, where you go, what you wear, how you treat people, what you buy, and it even controls the condition of your physical body.

* Thoughts are seeds and when planted in the mind, then cultivated and watered will bring forth a harvest.

2
Overcoming Obstacles

Success is to be measured not so much by the position that one has reached in life as by the obstacles which he has overcome.
~Booker T. Washington

An obstacle, also referred to as a barrier or stumbling block is anything that causes an obstruction. This may include an object, a thing, an action or a situation. Every human being on earth has faced some kind of problem, adversity, hindrance, or challenge, but the way in which we face these stumbling blocks greatly determines the outcome of them. Never was it ever written, stated, or directly told that we would never have any problems in life. The wealthiest people on earth have problems and face obstacles, so do the most famous, the most powerful, and even the royal families have problems and have faced obstacles. Everyone has their share. If the road to success were easy, everyone would travel it quickly and without difficulty. Even if you have been diligent in setting your goals, working on action plans for the attainment of your goals, and have worked consistently at your plan, there will still be obstacles in the path along the way. It is the joy and journey of clearing those obstacles that makes life meaningful and helps you feel truly gratified when you finally do reach your pinnacle of success. Obstacles will show up. That's a given, but the goal is not how to prevent them, but how to overcome them. Recognizing what kind of obstacle you are facing helps you to realize just how much power you have over it. In other words, there are external obstacles, internal obstacles, and habitual obstacles. External obstacles are things such as the economy, natural disasters, physical limitations, few job opportunities, the political climate, and/or other people's actions, etc. They are things in life that you have no control over. They get in the way of you building the life you want and accomplishing your goals within your desired timeframe. With these as obstacles, you must find the best solution to work your way around them. When you use the power of your mind, an answer for how to overcome these types of obstacles will come. Internal obstacles are usually those that you can control. These can be referred to as negative thinking, your belief system, unforgiveness, invisible walls, low self-esteem, shame, guilt, etc. All of these can be dealt with and overcome by way of a conscious effort and self-discipline. It is not easy, but can be done. Many times people do not realize that the outside problems they face are nothing more than their inside obstacles that have manifested in their environment. Habitual obstacles consist of bad habits that we do (or don't do) on a daily basis that cause us to not accomplish what we should accomplish in a timely manner. These types of obstacles can only be removed with a behavioral change.

    Always expect and prepare for the best, but do not be blindsided when you run into obstacles. Taking this perspective to life keeps you balanced. Obstacles are designed to give you a message or teach you a lesson. Just like pain, which serves as a signal that something is wrong somewhere in the body, obstacles serve as a signal to help you see that you may be going in the wrong direction. In other cases, obstacles are presented to test the level of your commitment to your vision. Whatever the reason, it is important that you refocus, regroup, and decide which approach you will take to handle it, then overcome it. You can either go over, around, or through your obstacle. It is all up to you.

External Obstacles

As stated, external obstacles are things that happen outside of our realm of control. With some external obstacles, such as natural disasters, death, physical limitations, or the political climate, there is a zero percent possibility that we can change what has happened. In these instances, we must simply develop a new game plan in place of the one that has been obstructed and try reaching the goal from another direction. In cases where this is not possible, then look at it as a blessing that you were definitely going in the wrong direction and this obstacle was indirectly designed to get you on the right course. Your life has been predestined from the foundation of the world and He sends signs, signals and messages constantly, which guide us back on the right track. We must simply tune in to listen, then follow the leading. There are some external obstacles that we do have some degree of control over, though not a lot. In other words, if your ability to do certain things is limited because you do not have a job and the job opportunities are limited, then you must continue to search for a job until one is secured. Giving up is certainly not an option, so until you find a job, you have no control over your obstacle, but your realm of control is when you are diligent in looking and consistent in trying to find one. In a situation where the obstacle is someone else's attitude and actions, you cannot control them, but you have some degree of control in the situation when it comes to how you respond to them. You can choose to respond negatively to their actions or you can respond positively. Of course, if you respond negatively, the situation will only get worse, but if your response is calm and somewhat positive, the situation may get better. No, you cannot control other people's behavior, but you can control your own, and as a result, the other person may alter their behavior, response, or decision towards you.

Internal Obstacles

Overcoming internal barriers can be hard and takes lots of time and effort because oftentimes people do not realize that it's their own internal issues that are the obstacles preventing them from moving forward. Everyone has some internal baggage which has resulted from the things they have experienced in life, but the key is not to allow them to control and dictate your life. When internal baggage has not been appropriately dealt with, it seeps out little by little and sabotages your goals, aspirations, and dreams. In order to gain mastery over the internal obstacles that may be blocking you from moving forward, you must recognize what they are and admit that you have them. Recognition is the first step; otherwise those obstacles will remain.

People behave as a result of what they have seen, heard, experienced, and been through in life, but regardless of what you have gone through, you are in control of your own behavior. People look at how others behave and draw their own conclusions about them. Most times, people do not consider what you may have been through as a reason for your (negative or inappropriate) disposition. They just observe the behavior, make a judgment about you, then treat you accordingly. One of the best ways to overcome an internal barrier is to move forward positively in our actions regardless of what is being experienced on the inside. This is certainly not to say to ignore what is being felt on the inside, because those issues must be dealt with, but the world does not have to know that we are angry, bitter, hurt or guilty through our actions. We must relegate our actions in spite of our feelings and emotions. Relegating the actions on the outside will change the thinking on the inside at the moment. The more you do this, the less those hindering emotions and thoughts will feel like barriers. Eventually, they will be overcome.

Habitual Obstacles

Webster's Dictionary defines a habit as any act performed so often that it becomes automatic. If you consider a frequent action to be unpleasant and it has no benefit for you, then it is labeled a bad habit (i.e. lateness, oversleeping, thinking or speaking negatively, smoking, using profanity, wasting time, etc.). Some bad habits are blatantly obvious, such as the ones mentioned above, but there are others that are more subtle, but can actually hinder forward-moving progress in life. These may include, but are not limited to, negative thinking, procrastinating, lack of follow-through, self-doubt, etc. In order to discover our subtle bad habits, we must become more cognizant of ourselves, our behaviors, what motivates us and what demotivates us. Being cognizant of these will help to discover our habitual obstacles.

No major accomplishment ever came easy. If it did, the self-gratification that accompanies the reward wouldn't be felt. To acquire wisdom and strength of character, we need obstacles to overcome, adversities to get through, and tests to pass. These build character and strengthen the perseverance in us. It is helpful to know what some of the major obstacles in life are. The ones identified below are the most common with which people struggle. I have identified five for you. Let's explore them:

Obstacle #1: Fear

Fear is what keeps many people from achieving and pursuing massive goals that God has given them the ability to accomplish. They have capability, the skills, and the intellectual wherewithal to take their innate gifts to great heights of achievement, but fear keeps them from moving forward. In Webster's dictionary, fear is defined as, *an unpleasant, sometimes strong emotion caused by an anticipation or awareness of danger or anxious concern.* Fear can also be defined as an *unpleasant, sometimes strong emotion caused by the anticipation of loss.* People fail to realize that when you fear something so badly, you actually bring the very thing that you fear into your life. The strong energy that is put towards the thought of what you fear magnifies the thing and brings it into fruition. It does not matter what thoughts you entertain. If you entertain them long enough, and put enough thought energy into them, they will manifest at the first opportunity to do so. Power flows where energy goes. Where is your energy flowing? You must get rid of all hindering, negative thoughts of doubt and fear. What you think about, you bring about, and what you think about the longest, becomes the strongest. Psychologists say that human beings are born with two types of fear: the fear of falling, and the fear of loud noises. All other fears are learned. They come with knowledge or develop as a result of our experiences. They come from what we are taught or what we hear and see. In his book, *The Magic of Thinking Big*, Author David Schwartz, Ph.D, writes on the subject of fear, the following:

> *Fear is real, and we must recognize it exists before we can conquer it... Fear stops people from capitalizing on opportunity; fear wears down physical vitality; fear actually makes people sick; causes organic difficulties, shortens life; and closes your mouth when you want to speak... Action cures fear. Indecision and postponement fertilize fear...Hesitation enlarges and magnifies fear... To overcome fear, act. To feed fear, wait, put off, postpone... the only cure for fear, is action.*

Either you will conquer fear or fear will conquer you. Oftentimes the only thing that holds us back from accomplishing great things is our fear - fear of failure, fear of what people might say or think, fear of how we are going to make it financially, and believe it or not, fear of success. When you overcome your fears, great and powerful things begin to happen. The most liberating, yet surprising thing about fear is that when you finally do overcome your fears, you realize that they were not as big as you made yourself think they were. I once saw an acronym for the word fear that is applicable to this subject:

F E A R:
False **E**xpectations **A**ppearing **R**eal.

Once you overcome your "false expectations" and pursue your goals with complete faith in yourself, you will begin doing things you never imagined were possible. Your greatest crises will come from the fear of trouble, not from the presence of trouble. The spirit of fear will bring terror to a person's deathbed. Like a virus, fear invades the soul, looking for filth upon which it may feed. Disease has killed its thousands, but the spirit of fear has killed its tens of thousands. Fearlessness removes all fear. One of the most profound writings on fear that I have ever read comes from Marianne Williamson in the following:

> *Our deepest fear is not that we are inadequate. Our deepest fear is that we are powerful beyond measure. It is our light, not our darkness that most frightens us. We ask ourselves, "Who am I to be brilliant, gorgeous, talented, and fabulous?" Actually, who are you not to be? You are a child of God. Your playing small does not serve the world. There is nothing enlightened about shrinking so that other people won't feel insecure around you. We are all meant to shine, as children do. We were born to make manifest the glory of God that is within us. It's not just in some of us; it's in everyone. And as we let our own light shine, we unconsciously give other people permission to do the same. As we are liberated from our own fear, our presence automatically liberates others.*

Wow, how liberating is that? If the words in her writing doesn't at least compel you to want to conquer fear, then I'm not sure what will. Fear will never accomplish anything because it is a paralyzer. If you allow fear to sneak in, then your purpose, your energy, and your power all cease.

Obstacle #2: Lack of self-confidence

The lives of many people are limited because they carry around self-defeating beliefs about themselves which cause them to have low self-esteem and little confidence. They do not know who they really are and therefore do not walk in the level of confidence they need in order to make a significant impact in this world.

Confidence depends upon the type of thoughts about yourself that you habitually allow to occupy your mind. When you think defeat, you are bound to feel defeated. Therefore, the degree to which you reprogram yourself from false beliefs will be in direct proportion to the amount of truth that you are willing to accept about yourself. You must gain self-confidence through self-reliance and self-approval.

People are drawn to people who have confidence because they desire it too. Confidence attracts. No normal person is drawn to a person with low self-esteem regardless of how beautiful or handsome they may be. With low self-esteem, you cannot positively contribute to anyone's life because that which you do, comes from wanting acceptance and validation from others. People with low self-esteem withdraw from other people to the point that it becomes draining. You do not need to seek approval from others. The only approval you need is God's approval. Be the type of person who pours into the lives of others in a positive way. True confidence comes from knowing that you are worthy and deserving of the things you desire, and through self-reliance, you pursue them. Adopt an attitude that anything is possible and recognize that it is possible because you deserve it and are worthy of it. You must believe and know that the whole universe is on your side. No one is against you - not the universe, not situations, not people, not God. God is always for you giving you the ability to choose rightly. When you deal with the enemy on the inside, you simultaneously deal with the enemy on the outside. Change your perspective about things. Look at the silver lining, not the black cloud. Don't curse the darkness. Light a candle and the darkness will vanish. Everything goes back to beliefs, thoughts, and words. Make sure that the thoughts you entertain aren't negative and self-defeating, which minimizes your self-confidence. As with anything else, you can increase your self-confidence on a daily basis with practice. The following are some techniques that you can do to practice being confident:

- Be secure in your conversations and give eye contact.

- Be clear and knowledgeable when speaking to others. Know what you are talking about, and convey that knowledge in a self-assured way.

- Walk with your back straight and your head held high. Typically, people with low self-esteem walk a little slower than most people and often keep their head looking down. A head that is held high is a sign of self confidence.

- Initiate conversations when it is appropriate to do so. Introduce yourself to people and engage in positive discussions.

- Dress in a manner that says you are important and are to be respected. Stay well-groomed.

- Speak out when it is necessary to do so (only when it's necessary).

- Never let anyone mistreat you. Stand up for yourself.

- Do not compromise your integrity. Hold on to your virtues. Always be ethical and remain honest.

With self-confidence, you draw a different caliber of people to you. You begin to feel good about yourself and your thinking process changes for the better. Practice confidence and your fears and insecurities will soon vanish.

Obstacle #3: Toxic Relationships

A toxic relationship can be defined as constant interaction with someone who is detrimental to your mindset, health, success, image and well-being. These interactions are not limited to intimate relationships only, but may also include so-called friendships, acquaintances, family members, negative work environments, business dealings, as well as boyfriend/girlfriend and/or husband/wife relationships. The very word "toxic" means deadly, poisonous, lethal, venomous, or fatal to your health and well-being. Toxic relationships serve as obstacles to your success. Oftentimes people do not realize they have toxic relationships in their lives because they are so use to them that they do not recognize them as toxic. For them, they are a part of life. These people have simply resolved in their mind, *"That's just the way he or she is"* but the truth of the matter is that just because someone in your life is negative, you do not have to allow that negativism into your sphere. These relationships serve as hindrances to where you are trying to go. Toxic relationships are like a ball and chain connected to your ankle, making it very difficult to take the next step forward. It's difficult I know, when you live in the same household with a toxic person, or when you must work with them, but you do not have to allow them into your mental sphere. You can resolve in your mind that there is no place for their negativity in your positive, elevating mind, and therefore you will not entertain any negativity that comes from them. When they finish with their pessimism, you simply dismiss it mentally and rub off any residue of it like water from a duck's back. It is simply a matter of mental strength and mind control. Eliminating toxic folks out of your life when they do not live with you is a bit easier because it's simply a matter of decision. It is true that you somewhat become like those you are with the most, so as you strive to go higher in mind, which will take you higher in life, you must watch whose around you. Analyze the energy they give off and decide if they are a help or a hindrance to you moving forward. There is no way that you can be around negative people for long without picking up some of their negativism. It is essential that you carefully choose the people you decide to allow into your inner sphere/circle. People come into your life to add, subtract, multiply, or divide. Review those in your life to make sure they are adding to you as a better person, not subtracting from your vigor, strength, and positive energy. You definitely want to separate from people who are causing division between you and others. You want those in your life who will help to multiply your gifts, talents, skills, and abilities. The wrong people can hold you back, drag you down, and drain you of your creative energy. People come to you as an appointment or a dis-appointment. You can only move forward with the right people around you. Toxic associations will eventually corrupt a good character.

 Most grocery items have a shelf life, and if you consume the food beyond the expiration date, chances are that you will get sick. Things and people in your life also have an expiration date. Keeping them longer than you are supposed to could make you sick and weak. Some of your friends and/or acquaintances are fine for where you are now, but not for where you are going. As you rise to another level and into another dimension of success, they cannot go. In order to gain something, you must give up something. Toxic people cannot handle where you are going and they will try to (either consciously or subconsciously) hinder you from moving forward. Get rid of them. The space left by them will be filled with a different caliber of people that will help propel you for where God is taking you. Replace toxic people with progressive people. Progressive people are positive, innovative, and forward-thinking. Connecting yourself with the right people will help to expand your mindset and raise you up to the level they are. You cannot get to the millionaire level with a hundred dollar mindset. You cannot get to the apostle level with a pastor's mindset. You cannot be on the board of directors with a blue collar mindset, and you cannot get to the place where you are being chauffeured in a limousine if you are still hanging out with your friends on the bus stop. There is a great benefit in sitting under the tutelage of the great. If you have millionaires as friends, it's because you are on your way to becoming one. The people you hang around will help to expand your mindset. The company you keep matters. If you are the smartest person among your friends, then you need a new set of friends.

Toxic people have characteristics that are hard to hide. If someone you are close with displays certain personality traits that are questionable, then it is time to dig a little deeper and make some decisions. Some of these traits may include being verbally abusive, dishonest, negative, competitive, controlling, critical, insecure, jealous, lazy, or pessimistic. This is a short list. It isn't hard to distinguish positive traits from negative ones. Just keep in mind that toxic people serve as obstacles to your success, so in your pursuit of greatness, you may need to do some purging.

Obstacle #4: Careless Speaking

The tongue is a powerful tool that can be used for good or evil. Most people are mentally lazy and allow their minds to think, and their mouths to speak whatever they want. When you do not understand the power that is in your mouth, you are ignorant to the principle of speaking things into existence. Some people are so careless with their words that they are constantly creating the circumstances around them for the worse. Just as thoughts are things, words are things. The thoughts that you think manifest into the things that you see in your life; and the words that you speak create the circumstances that you experience in your life. In other words, we can speak life into a situation and change it for the better or we can speak death into a situation and change it for the worse. Those who have wisdom realize the power that their words carry, and therefore they use their words strategically and carefully. They say nothing that they do not want to see manifested into their lives. We would be wise to do the same.

Obstacle #5: A Negative Attitude

Your attitude is seen by everyone without you saying a word. Your attitude often dictates the circumstances you find yourself in, and your attitude may also determine how you get out of circumstances. Attitudes reflect thinking. How we think shows on our faces. If we are happy, it shows. If we are sad, it shows. If we are angry, it shows. If we are embarrassed about something, it shows. Not only does attitude show through facial expressions, but attitudes are also exhibited through our actions. Attitudes are nothing but mirrors of the mind because they reflect what we are thinking. Without opening your mouth, others can usually tell what kinds of thoughts you are thinking based upon your body movements, behaviors, actions, and disposition. You choose your attitude every morning when you get up. Your attitude when you wake up sets the tone for the rest of your day. What attitude did you choose this morning? Was it, "Good morning Lord!" or was it, "GOOD LORD, IT'S MORNING!" The human attitude is the advance person of your true self. The root of your attitude is hidden, but the fruit is always visible. When it comes to success, your attitude will determine your decision to try again. When you embrace a positive attitude, you are determined to succeed no matter what. Those who embrace a positive attitude look at failure as a signal to streamline their efforts. When they have tried something major and failed at it, they try again. Failure is not an option for the determined. If you started a business and it failed, try again! If you ran for public office and lost, try again! If you applied for a promotion and didn't get it, try again! If you pitched your idea to a major organization and they rejected it, try again! The most successful people in the world are those who refused to give up when they failed. Only those who endure to the end get the prize. Temporary defeat is not permanent failure. Just dust yourself off and try again! When a positive attitude becomes a way of life, you simply cannot fail.

Attitudes are revealed in how we act, and how we act, determines how others react towards us. Your attitude can be your best friend or your worst enemy. It draws people to you or repels people from you. A positive attitude will win you favor, but a negative one will earn you foes. You can have all the money in the world, but if you have a negative disposition, you will turn many people off. I once heard this quote that really gives consideration to the benefits of having a positive attitude: *"Even if you don't have money, if you have a positive attitude and good manners, they can take you all over the world."* Good manners and a positive attitude are like sugar that attracts bees to honey. People read attitudes through body language, voice tones, and inflections. We must realize the impact that our attitude has on every kind of relationship in our lives. When the attitude is right, our abilities reach a maximum of effectiveness and good results inevitably follow. Winston Churchill wrote, *"Attitude is a little thing that makes a big difference."* The ability to maintain a positive attitude, especially in the midst of challenges, is an asset that can never be measured. Essentially, your attitude will determine your success in life. Maintaining a positive attitude is about choices in emotional responses. People with this ability choose their focus instead of allowing circumstances to dictate their emotions. These positive people tend to remain in a rational state of mind, and make the most of whatever life offers them. They know how to seize the day and create good memories by projecting a positive future through their attitude. They solve problems as quickly as possible when they can. They often do more, go further, and experience more enjoyable, fulfilling and satisfying lives. Albert Einstein quoted the following as it pertains to attitude. This quote sums up the whole matter on the subject: *"Weakness of attitude becomes weakness of character."* Watch your attitude!

    In considering what has been written in this chapter about obstacles, it behooves us to embrace them when they arrive and use them as stepping stones to greatness. Obstacles come for various reasons, but the way in which we get around, over, or through them will determine the mental strength and character that is gained from overcoming. Self-gratification is not found in the destination. It is found in the journey. The road to success will not be a smooth one

Overcoming Obstacles

having no bumps in the road. There will be some bumps, rainy days, detours, roadblocks and obstacles, but if you keep your eye on the map and focus on your destination, you will arrive there safely, and when you do, you will appreciate all the obstacles you endured along the way.

Success Keys

* The wealthiest people on earth have obstacles; so do the most famous, the most powerful and even royal families have problems and face obstacles.

* Obstacles will show up. The goal is not how to prevent obstacles, but how to overcome them.

* God has predestined your life from the foundation of the world and He sends signs, signals and messages to us constantly, which guide us back on the right track. We must simply tune in to listen, then follow the leading.

* You must get rid of all hindering, negative thoughts of doubt and fear. What you think about, you bring about and what you think about the longest, becomes the strongest.

* The lives of many people are limited because they carry around self-defeating beliefs about themselves which cause them to have low self-esteem and little confidence.

3
Self & Self-discipline

Self-discipline is an act of cultivation. It requires you to connect today's actions to tomorrow's results. ~Gary Ryan Blair

The successful life is a disciplined life. True success is not a one-time event. It is a life-long journey that comes to those who plan and prepare, to those who are persistent, and to those who are willing to endure the pain of self-discipline to achieve their goals. Self-discipline has many definition variations, but the one that defines it the most to me is, *the ability to get yourself to take action regardless of your emotional state of mind; the ability to forgo instant and immediate gratification and pleasure in favor of a greater gain or more satisfying result.* Essentially, self-discipline requires sacrifice and self-denial. These are the difference between the lazy and the hardworking. Successful people are hardworking. They take time to do things that mentally lazy people do not like to do. While mentally lazy people are wasting hours watching useless television shows, the self-disciplined person uses those same hours doing things that will bring them closer to the fulfillment of their goals. These may include such things as studying to pass an exam, developing a business plan, writing a book, researching information in their field, working on their website, preparing for a presentation, making business phone calls, developing a seminar, exercising, etc. Lack of self-discipline contributes significantly to mediocrity, failure, and even sometimes poverty. I say again, the successful life is a disciplined life! Self-discipline ripens the understanding and arouses an activity of mind and keenness of perception that prepares you for sustainable success. Most people live in mediocrity or slightly above or below it because they are too mentally lazy to put forth the self-discipline necessary to find the road out of lack and limitation and travel it.

Self-discipline appears in various forms, such as commitment, consistency, perseverance, restraint, endurance, thinking before acting, finishing what you start, and the ability to carry out decisions in spite of hardships. Self-discipline may also mean self-control, but it entails so much more. True self-discipline is the expression of inner strength and power, which is vital for dealing with the affairs of daily life and for the achieving of goals. A self- disciplined person is one who understands "self" and how to enhance and strengthen their inner self. There are many sides to self that should be explored because if you do not understand self, how can you understand anyone else? Self-discipline and self-control are Siamese twins and they have relatives in their family that are just as important as they are. Let us explore some of their family members.

Self-initiative

The term "self" always has to do with YOU. Self is all about what makes YOU the person you are: YOUR personality, YOUR thoughts, YOUR behaviors, YOUR actions, etc. The term "initiative" means doing things without having to be told or the act of starting something; therefore self-initiative means doing things without anyone telling you to do them. Fundamentally, it means to be proactive. Self-initiative is the opposite of procrastination. The power of initiative is the critical catalyst for personal achievement.

A person with initiative is motivated to do things in a timely manner. When you take the initiative to develop goals for your life, then work on accomplishing those goals, you have applied the principle of self-initiative. Those who have this attribute are not afraid to take the first step and start before others. They are people of vision. Without personal initiative, you will never start anything. You need it in order to make your dreams a reality. Got self-initiative?

Self-awareness

Self-awareness is the conscious perception of knowing what your capabilities are, the dynamics of your personality, your strengths, weaknesses, fears, habits, motivations, thoughts, actions, and emotions. More often than not, a person who is self-aware tends to also be self-disciplined and exercises a higher degree of self-control than most people. Self-aware individuals are observant and because they have spent time analyzing themselves, they are inclined to have a better understanding of the actions of others. As people become more aware of themselves and their innate tendencies and predispositions, they begin also watching their thought patterns. This leads them to notice the connection between their thoughts and actions. They become masterminders, in that they begin to master their mind. Introspection, which

> *Self-aware individuals are observant and because they have spent time analyzing themselves.*

means the examining of one's thoughts, feelings, and behaviors, plays a major role in self-awareness. One cannot be self-aware without going within.

Through application of this characteristic, you see where your thoughts and emotions are taking you so that you can cling to what is usefully beneficial and filter what is not. Having self-awareness is to possess a valuable attribute that brings beneficial returns. This trait enables you to turn inward which forces you to evaluate, change, or manage your emotions. The scrutiny will not always be pleasant, but the ability to recognize the negativity gives you the power to release them. Being aware of, and recognizing shortcomings, faults, vices, defects and ugliness can be a humbling experience, but the reward is greater than the temporary blow to the ego. Those negative elements are nothing more than weaknesses that can be turned into strengths. Once you realize what needs changing, you can make the decision to take action. You are then on course to becoming a better and greater person. Got self-awareness?

Self-respect

Self-respect is having love, admiration, pride, and confidence in yourself. When you respect yourself, you are self-assured in your worth and you project an image that commands the respect of others. When you respect yourself, you are strategic with your words and actions, knowing that what you speak, sends a message to people about the caliber of person you are. When you respect yourself, you do not allow others to treat you any kind of way, because you carry yourself in a manner that silently speaks a message to the world that, *"I am a person of worth and I expect you to respect me."* This is not having a false sense of self-worth, but a realization that through self-awareness, you are worthy of respect. You understand that as you respect others, they will respect you. People who respect themselves have various types of personalities. Some are introverted; some are extroverted. Some are highly intellectual; some have average intellect. Some are overachievers, some are mediocre. Achievement has very little to do with self-respect. A poor person can have self-respect while a rich person has very little. Self-respect comes from belief systems, values, standards, morals, ethics and integrity. How much value you place on each of these determines how much of them you are willing to embrace. People with self-respect take pride in their deportment, their manners and also their image. For the most part, they are pretty level-headed when it comes to temperament. They realize that the loss of self-control reveals a weakness in character, so they try hard to maintain composure at all times. With self-respect, it is easy to cultivate and enhance the other "self" attributes that you will be reading about on the next few pages. Got self-respect?

Self-reliance

To be self-reliant inherent means to "rely on self." The catalytic word that comes from self-reliance is independence. Self-reliant people rarely depend upon others to do for them what they can do for themselves. They take the bull by the horn and make things happen. If they see no opportunities to seize, they *make* opportunities for themselves. Self-reliant people realize that in order to achieve any level of success, they must take initiative. They work hard and utilize available resources in order to achieve a beneficial outcome. These people tend to be forward-thinkers, visionaries, and quick decision-makers. They are fully aware of their strengths and weaknesses and rely upon themselves to overcome their impediments. Children should be taught to be self-reliant in their toddler years. When parents fail to allow children to earn what they desire or when they do for the children what the children can do for themselves, they are failing to teach them self-reliance. They are instilling in them a sense of entitlement and they grow up relying on others to do for them what they should have been taught to do for themselves. When parents think they are being good parents by giving, giving, giving, they are actually doing more harm than good. When self-reliance is taught and instilled, it is likened to teaching a child how to fish, rather than just giving them fish to eat. Self-reliance will help children become self-sustaining adults. This trait is especially needful for men, who are expected to be able to provide for the household. A sense of pride emerges in the self-reliant person who has earned his or her way to success without having to rely on others for favors or handouts. Of course, we need others to rely on in various other areas, but we should not need others to do for us what we can do on our own. Self-gratification gravitates to the self-reliant person after goals are achieved. Got self-reliance?

Self-efficacy

Self-efficacy is defined as how a person feels about their personal abilities. It is their own "I can" or "I cannot" belief in themselves. Self-efficacy beliefs begin to form in early childhood as children deal, and are successful with a wide variety of experiences, tasks, and situations. Self-efficacy has a lot to do with self-confidence. The very word *efficacy* means the ability to be able to produce an "effect", in other words, it is your belief in how effectual you think you can be. We all have self-efficacy about various aspects of our lives. In other words, our self-efficacy in one area may be extremely high and in another area, it may be low. Self-efficacy in a specific area is specific to the task being attempted. A boy may have high self-efficacy in the area of football, but low self-efficacy in the area of basketball. A girl may have high self-efficacy in the area of singing, but low self-efficacy in the area of drawing.

With a high self-efficacy comes a high self-confidence in a particular area. Self-efficacy determines what goals you pursue, how much effort you put forth towards attaining those goals, how persistent you are in the face of obstacles, and the difficulty of the goals you set. The connection between self-efficacy and achievement gets stronger as you accomplish one goal after the next. With self-efficacy, you recover quickly from setbacks and continue to persevere in spite of obstacles. Self-efficacy plays a major role in how goals, tasks, and challenges are approached. Got self-efficacy?

Self-esteem

Success begins with self-esteem. Self-esteem has to do with self-worth. It is a person's estimated value placed on themselves. It is a judgment and attitude consisting of positive or negative evaluations regarding how a person truly feels about themselves. People with self-esteem issues are always looking for acceptance and validation from others. They are affected by the way others treat them. If people treat them well, they feel good. If they are not treated well, their feelings are hurt and they sometimes become depressed, pondering over and over in their minds what they could have done that caused that person not to like them. Their sense of worth comes from other people accepting them. The more positive your thoughts and feelings about yourself are, the higher your self-esteem will be. On the contrary, the more negative your thoughts and feelings about yourself are, the lower your self-esteem will be. Feeling good about yourself is imperative, because it gives you a sense of power over your own life, helps you to be satisfied in relationships, allows you to set realistic expectations, and enables you to pursue your *own* goals. Focusing on your skills, gifts, talents, and abilities is a good way of increasing self-esteem. When you work in the area that makes you shine, your self-esteem will surely increase.

Placing a high value on yourself gives you the motivation required to achieve your own goals. When your self-esteem is high, you do not need, nor do you seek to be validated from others. Being accepted or praised is not something that is craved by those with high esteem because their validation comes from personal achievement. Having low esteem on the other hand, contributes to a distorted view of who you really are, and a distorted view of how you see others. People with high self-esteem focus on goal-setting, personal growth, and advancing in life. Those with low self-esteem focus on other people, fitting in, and being accepted. A sure way to increase self-esteem is by setting and achieving goals. Goals give long-term vision, which creates the motivation to achieve them. Got self-esteem?

Self-gratification

Gratification is the pleasurable feeling of pride that emerges from goal-attainment. Self-gratification emerges when through hard work, effort, sacrifice, and labor, you finally accomplish the goals you have set. Gratification cannot be manufactured. It springs up from the inside of a person when they have earned something, and will not emerge when a desire has been secured through dishonest, selfish, or deceitful means. A false, superficial feeling of self-gratification may be embraced, but true gratification, which is a gift from our Maker for hard work and toil will not come to the one who has not truly earned what they have received. Gratification may come from all types of achievement. In other words, the doctoral student who is awarded a Ph.D experiences the self-gratifying feeling from having worked so hard to achieve that impressive goal. By the same token, the college student who earns his or her two-year associates degree also experiences the self-gratifying feeling from having worked hard. Their achievements may be on different levels, but the same self-gratification emerges because they both worked hard for what they earned, and therefore, are both self-gratified. There is no feeling like that of self-gratification, and the desire to experience it gives motivation for pursuing other goals. Self-gratification significantly contributes to self-esteem because it increases self-worth.

Given that self-esteem has to do with feelings of worthiness, self-gratification inevitably helps to increase self-worth. As long as you work towards goals that are worthy, meaningful, and important to you, then self-gratification will be felt when you accomplish those goals. This feeling may come from various achievements on a litany of scales including, but not limited to: graduating from high school or college, getting married, having children, getting promoted, writing a book, starting a business, putting together an event, program or seminar, or may even come from buying a new car or home. Short-term gratification may emerge from such things such as winning a basketball game, passing an exam, submitting a report on time, doing a great job on a project or even paying your bills on time. Got self-gratification?

Self-actualization

To self-actualize means to reach your full potential. I first heard the term "self-actualization" as an undergraduate student working on a Bachelor's Degree. I then ran across the term again in graduate school. Understanding the full meaning of the term, I am forever seeking to reach self-actualization. The term was brought to prominence by a psychologist named Abraham Maslow when he connected self-actualization to what he called his hierarchy of needs for human beings. According to Maslow, all humans go through a continuum of steps in life, and as one step is mastered, we progress to the next step, the last being that of self-actualization. Each step must be achieved first before going on to the next step. There is a 5-step process in the hierarchy and they must be achieved in order:

1. physiological (food, shelter, water, basic needs)
2. safety (health, employment, family, social stability)
3. love and belonging (loving someone, being loved by others, being connected to organizations, status, responsibility)
4. self-esteem (self-worth, being accepted, confidence, recognition, respect)
5. self-actualization (fulfillment, manifestation of full potential)

Each step must be mastered in the hierarchy before you can effectively proceed to the next level. The previous step must be fully mastered before moving forward. In other words, how can self-esteem (step 2) be achieved if one is concerned with where their next meal is coming from (step 1)? How can a person be interested in being accepted into an organization (step 3), if their health is failing (step 2)? In order to effectuate each step of the hierarchy, the step before has to be fully mastered. The main thing to understand about self-actualization is that it is a process not a goal. We should always be striving to self-actualize.

You have just read about some of the family members of the twins, self-discipline, and self-control. As you can see, the "self"

Self & Self-Discipline

family comes from quality and excellence, each having great assets and beneficial results. The matriarch of the family is self-actualization. However, although you've met the dignified and prominent family members, I think it is equally important that you meet the black sheep of the family in order to avoid them when you see them approaching. They are trouble and can lead you down a very lonely and destructive path. Let's meet them now:

Self-doubt

To be connected with self-doubt is to be uncertain, undecided, or inclined to disbelieve positive things about yourself and your abilities. Self-doubt is closely connected to low self-esteem because with low self-esteem, you've placed little worth on yourself. You doubt your capabilities in certain areas and therefore shy away from those areas. Self-doubt is the opposite of self-confidence. One cannot be present if the other is present. The two never coincide or dwell together. Self-doubt causes procrastination, indecision, delay, and/or hesitation. We all have self-doubt in some areas of our lives. It is human nature to be doubtful in the areas we are less skillful in, but self-doubt becomes a hindrance when it interferes with pursuing goals, making important decisions, or performing effectively when you have the ability to do so.

When there is an absence or lack of self-confidence, self-doubt emerges. Self-doubt is certain to paralyze anyone desirous of elevating their lives by taking faith leaps into new and positive ventures. Self-doubt will cause a boy to lose the girl he likes to his friend because the friend had the confidence to strike up a conversation when the boy doubted himself and feared rejection. Self-doubt can cause your colleague to get a promotion over you, even though you were better qualified; but since you doubted that you would be chosen, you did not apply for the position and your friend did. It is the bold and confident who succeed in life. You must get rid of self-doubt and replace it with self-confidence! Got self-doubt? Get rid of it!

Self-hatred

Self-hatred is the family member from which all the others stay away. It is a deeply rooted dislike for self and may have emanated from a variety of reasons. People who posses this element have negative thoughts, destructive behaviors, bizarre actions, and usually have a dislike for people they wish they could be like. The root cause of self-hatred is specific to each individual, but may have emerged because of some form of abuse (sexual, verbal, physical), emotional trauma, wrong things done in the past, neglect to do something that should or could have done, failed relationships, failed endeavors and/or a distorted view of life in general. These people give off a negative vibration which magnetizes more negativity back to them, thus feeding their hatred for themselves. Needless-to-say, their self-image and self-worth is low and they are often depressed because of their current position. The inability to separate themselves from themselves increases frustration, and their self-sabotaging behaviors destroy any good that they would do. These individuals have a very hard time accepting praises and/or compliments and immediately respond with a negative reply when a compliment is given. Unforgiveness of self and others plays a big role in self-hatred when the loathing comes from a wrong done by them or to them in the past. When a person cannot find it within themselves to forgive themselves, it makes moving forward extremely difficult. Their unforgiveness serves as a heavy burden, making it hard to pursue goals and embrace success.

Others have self-hatred because they have spent the majority of their lives trying to imitate others so much, that they do not know who they truly are. Instead of recognizing their uniqueness and embracing it, they have spent their time and energy trying to be someone they are not. Self-hatred leads to self-sabotage, which ultimately destroys a person. If the self-hatred element is something that you can identify with either in yourself or in others, then understand that this self-defeating impediment is something that can be destroyed. Below are some things that you can do to help eradicate this demon:

- Forgive yourself for any wrongs that you have done in the past that continue to haunt you. If it is in your ability to ask for forgiveness from the person/people you have wronged, do it. This will lift a heavy burden off of you. If they refuse to forgive you, then you must forgive yourself and move on.

- Forgive others for what they did to you.
    * Research from the 'Darkness to Light Organization' has shown that victims of molestation and other forms of abuse blame themselves for what was done to them. They reason within themselves that they must have deserved what happened to them because they are unworthy. This mindset must change. That justification is distorted and untrue.

- Understand that no amount of reason can excuse an abuse done to anyone. Everyone is responsible for their own actions. Resolve in your mind that despite how awful the abuse may have been, you will forgive and move on. If you refuse to forgive, you are allowing that person/people to still have control over you. Free yourself. Forgive and move on to the success that awaits you! You can do it!

- Identify the gifts and skills that you have and begin cultivating them. Whatever your skills are, do them as often as you can. They will get stronger and you will begin to feel better about yourself. If there is a way that you can benefit others with your gift, do it. Blessing others blesses you.

- Do random acts of kindness when it is in your ability to do so. This can range from paying for the coffee of the person behind you; helping someone take groceries to their car; buying someone a gift for no reason; giving up your seat for someone standing, etc. Good deeds always make the doer feel good about themselves, and lets the recipient of the good deed realize that there are still some good people out there. Acts of kindness are seeds that you plant and the harvest will always be good fruit.

- Be self-confident in who you are. Practice self-confidence by implementing the things on page 22. Find out what makes you unique from others and begin embracing that. Don't try to fit in where you don't belong. Be yourself and do not try to impress others. As you begin being you, others will gravitate to you.

- Smile more. When you walk by people, give a welcoming smile, and say hello. An intimidating look will keep others away. Watch your facial expressions. This is especially true for the "single and looking." If you are too serious, you might scare away a potential candidate.

- Watch your words and conversations. Refrain from speaking negatively about yourself and others. Stop complaining. Be thankful for the things you have. Remove yourself from pessimistic people. Begin to watch your words and speak only words that uplift, encourage, and support yourself and others.

- Speak positive affirmations, starting with yourself. "I am" affirmations begin to form your subconsciousness and shape your mindset. Before you know it, you will become who you say you are. Speaking positive will help to diminish a negative mindset.

As you have learned in this chapter, the "self" is made up of many components. Be sure that the majority of your "self formula" has good ingredients, because these will help you get to the top of the success latter. Stay away from those last two family members (self-doubt and self-hatred), and be aware of those who choose to hang around them or cling to them. In order to be all that you were destined to be, you must know who you are and what your strengths and weaknesses are. You know yourself better than anyone else, and as you strive to continue being the best person you can be, you will find that learning the true "self" frees you to be who you were created to be without putting on facades. You will love the true essence of who you are and that will propel you to the success level that you seek. Self-gratification will visit you often as you pursue and achieve one goal after the next.

Success Keys

* Lack of self-discipline contributes significantly to mediocrity, failure and even poverty. The successful life is a disciplined life.

* Self-aware individuals are observant and because they have spent time analyzing themselves, they are inclined to have a better understanding of the actions of others.

* Self-reliant people rarely depend upon others to do for them what they can do for themselves. They take the bull by the horn and make things happen. If they see no opportunities to seize, they make opportunities for themselves.

* Self-initiative is about you doing things without anyone telling you to do them. Essentially, it means being proactive. Self-initiative is the enemy of procrastination.

* Self-gratification emerges when, through hard work, effort, sacrifice and labor, you finally accomplish the goals you have set. Gratification cannot be manufactured. It springs up from inside of a person when they have earned it.

4
Strategic Goal-Setting

Learn from the past, set vivid, detailed goals for the future, and live in the only moment of time over which you have any control. NOW!

~Denis Waitley

You only have one life and it is up to you to live it the way you want. Life is a one-shot deal and you will get out of it what you put into it. There is no do-over with life. Since we know that life is what we make it, then why not plan your life as you would plan a vacation? Choose your destination, map out the steps needed to get you there safely, be ready when it's time to go, determine the best route to take to get there, and choose beforehand to enjoy both the journey and the destination once you arrive. I read in the 'Harvard Goal-setting Study' that only 3% of Americans write down their goals and actually strive to accomplish them. Three percent! This is because most of us go through life with goals, desires, and aspirations in our head, but we rarely think of putting them in writing and making them concrete. More often than not, people with written goals and action plans succeed in life, while people without them sometimes have no direction of how to get to their desired goal. If you have no goals to strive for and no plans for improving yourself, then what are you living for? What are you working towards? This is certainly not to say that people cannot be successful if they do not develop goals, but life is much more meaningful when you are striving to enhance your life and working towards goal attainment. Goals are like a road map in that they show you where you want to go. Planning tells you approximately how long it will take to get there. Plans are the "how" of goal setting. Plans delineate the steps you need to take along the way to arrive at your desired destination. For visual learners like me, you need to see things on paper. Not only does writing your goals down help to see clearly what it is that you aspire to do, have, and be, but seeing them written gives motivation for accomplishing them. Once you have taken the time and effort to write specifically what you want to achieve, the desire to accomplish them emerges from within you. There is power in putting pen to paper or keyboard to computer screen. A resurgence overwhelms you once you see your vision on paper; however, once those goals are on paper, you must not toss them aside never to look at them again. You must spend time examining and reviewing them frequently. Do not let your newfound motivation diminish. International Motivational Speaker Les Brown puts it this way in his book 'Live Your Dreams': *"With a powerful hunger for your dreams driving you, you will be surprised at the ideas that will come, at the people you will be able to attract, at the opportunities that will unfold. You will be able to see things that you won't believe you couldn't see before - things that may have been right there in front of you the whole time."* You have everything you need inside of you to accomplish your goals. The only thing that can stop you from pursuing them is YOU! You are the master of your own destiny. You are the captain of your ship.

Goal-setting techniques are used by highly successful people and achievers in all professions. Goals give you long-term vision and motivation. They organize your application of knowledge and help you to use your time wisely so that you can make the very best of your life. Remember to dream BIG! Norman Vincent Peale said it best when he stated in his book 'The Power of Positive Thinking' *When you affirm big, believe big, and pray big, big things happen.* Keep in mind that how big you think determines the size of your accomplishments. You can only achieve what you can see in your mind's eye. People who aim high and work towards accomplishing their goals are big visionaries. They are experts in creating positive, forward-looking, optimistic pictures in their minds, and in the minds of others. Do not concern yourself too much with *how* your goals will come into fruition after you have written an action plan for reaching them. Look at things not as they are, but as they can be. Visualization adds value to your aspirations. A big goal-setter always visualizes what can be done in the future. A big goal-setter is not concerned with the present. The challenge of competing with yourself and winning is self-gratifying. Don't give up. The reward is great if you persist until you succeed.

Properly setting goals can be incredibly motivating. As you get into the habit of setting and achieving goals, you will find that your self-confidence quickly increases. This is a sure way to increase self-esteem. In 1981, the acronym S.M.A.R.T. was introduced to the world to help give direction and meaning to goal-setting. Using the S.M.A.R.T. system when developing goals will help you to distinguish between solid goals and simple things-to-do. The essence of S.M.A.R.T. goals is to ensure that when you write them, they are **S**pecific, **M**easurable, **A**ction-oriented, **R**ealistic and **T**ime bound.

Traveling the Road to Success

S - Specific

When goals are broad, it makes obtaining them more challenging. Goals should be as specific and detailed as possible. When they are broken down into action plans, this helps with specificity.

M - Measurable

How are you going to measure your progress? In other words, how close are you to the achievement of the goal? 30%? 50%? 75%? You measure your achievement based upon how much more of the goal there is left to accomplish. Only you know how much longer you have to reach it.

A - ~~Attainable~~ Action Oriented

You may have seen S.M.A.R.T. goals before or will run across them after reading this. You will find that the "A" in S.M.**A.**R.T. originally stood for "attainable" but the two words realistic and attainable can be synonymous terms. Therefore, I used the new "Action Oriented" term to describe the "A". If you do not supplement your goals with action, you will never achieve anything. You must work at your goals each day through action and do something meaningful that will bring you closer to your desired goal.

Realistic

Your goals should be challenging, but also realistic. Setting goals that are virtually impossible to reach is fantasizing. You know what your capabilities are, how much of your intellectual wherewithal you can apply, and what is realistic enough for you to accomplish. To set a goal of becoming a judge in five years when you never went to law school (and have no intentions of going) is a fantasy not a goal. That is not realistic. Needless-to-say, commonsense and good judgment are needed when setting goals.

T - Time bound

It is imperative to have a timeline for accomplishing goals; otherwise, they can be carried over year after year. Every goal you set should have a targeted date of accomplishment. The dates may change because of priorities, detours or other things, but a realistic date should be attached to each goal that you have set.

When you use the S.M.A.R.T. method for developing your goals, you are very likely to have noteworthy, commendable, challenging goals that will definitely keep you on the road to success. However you decide to plan is up to you. The key is to plan. When you fail to plan, you plan to fail. The majority of people meet with failure in life because of their lack of persistence in creating new plans to take the place of the ones that have failed. When they do not see instant results, they become discouraged and quit. Stop hiding from success because you think you will fail. You *will* fail at some point on your journey. Failure is necessary. Your attitude determines your attainments. There will be some failure, but that is okay. Temporary defeat is not permanent failure. Some people will tell you "NO" along your journey to success. That's just fine. It is all part of the journey. Some will even tell you that your vision is too big and virtually impossible to achieve. That is fine too, because it gives you the motivation to prove them wrong, especially when you have solid action steps in place and you know your ability to be able to do it. Many of life's failures come from individuals who did not realize how close they were to success when they gave up. Success is not found in your circumstances. It is found in overcoming your circumstances. You cannot possess what you are unwilling to pursue. Even when you meet with failure, pursue success anyway. It is inside of you to succeed. No one succeeds without overcoming obstacles and opposition. The secret to becoming and remaining successful is to be like a duck, smooth and unruffled on the top, but paddling furiously underneath. Look at adversity like a lion looks at a juicy steak. He devours that steak as though it were his last meal. That is how you must look at adversity. Devour it and continue pursuing success. There would be no <u>test</u>imony if there were no <u>test</u>. Out of every adversity comes an equal or greater opportunity.

Personal Affirmation/Mission Statement

Before setting goals, I always begin by defining who I am and who I aspire to be. I call it my personal affirmation. Others call it their mission statement. They are essentially one in the same. I recite my affirmation at least twice per week to keep the words always in my subconsciousness. Your affirmation should be written in the present tense. It states your aspirations and goals as though they were already achieved. Words have power and as you speak your affirmation into the atmosphere, your words go out into the earth realm and return to you with astounding accuracy. You should want all of your desires to come into fruition, therefore you must speak them into existence!

An affirmation/personal mission statement is a snapshot of how you see yourself in the very near future. Some people have short ones, some have long ones, but what is most important is to have one for yourself. Once written, you are consciously aware of the person you aspire to be, and therefore are compelled to begin acting like that person. It is very real. From your affirmation/mission statement, will emerge your goals. Goals should be set in various areas of your life. These areas may include, but does not have to be limited to: spirituality, financial, educational, recreational, personal, family, business, community service, and/or health. Many people set goals in only a few of those areas, some cover each one listed. Others add their own category. It is all a matter of your own priorities and preferences.

Check and Balance

Your motivation is increased when you write your affirmation/mission statement. Writing an affirmation can be time consuming initially because it requires you to look deep inside yourself and identify your strengths and weaknesses. Going inside and bringing out the less attractive stuff can be a humbling, yet beneficial and worthwhile undertaking. It requires soul-searching. After writing your affirmation, your yearly goals will be easier to develop. Evaluate yourself and write down what you find out; then identify what you want out of life and what role you want to play in the lives of those with whom you love and interact. Once the mission statement and goals are written, there must be accountability. Frequently, you should review the goals that you have developed, then identify the smaller goals that you need to achieve in order to reach your large-scale goals. In doing this, recognize what is realistic enough to accomplish within a month's time.

> *Goal-setting may seem like a lot of work, but no one is going to put more time into your goals than you. Success is not easy. If it were, then everyone would be a success.*

Goal-setting may seem like a lot of work, but no one is going to put more time into your goals than you. Success is not easy. If it were, then everyone would be a success. There is a cost to be paid for it and this is part of the price you pay. When you want success bad enough, you must be willing to pay your dues to achieve it. The elevator to success is broken. You must take the stairs. In all human affairs, there are efforts and there are results, and the strength of the effort is the measure of the result. Nobody should care more about your life than you do.

Goals vs. Things to do

Many people confuse goals with things to do and it's easy to do if you are not careful. Basically, goals *are* "things to do" but the difference is that a goal is challenging and requires steps to accomplish. Things to do usually requires stopping long enough to make the time to do it. Things-to-do really do not require any sacrifice other than a sacrifice of time. For example, as you write your goals to achieve under the health category, your first one may be to lose 15 pounds. That is a challenging goal and it requires actions steps and self-discipline in order to accomplish it. However, your second health goal may be to remember to take your multivitamin each day. Goal #2 is NOT a goal. It is a "thing to do." The only sacrifice it requires is that of remembering, so in order to make sure you do not mix the two, ask yourself if what you have written requires steps and action plans. If it doesn't, then it may only be a "thing to do" which should go on your 'Thing to do' List, but not listed as a goal.

Short Term vs Long Term Goals

There are short-term goals and long-term goals that you will be making in the goal-setting process. Keep in mind that goal-setting is an ongoing, life-long process. You never arrive. You may take a break after achieving a noteworthy goal, but eventually, you must identify new goals to achieve. Oftentimes, those new goals are byproducts of the main goal that has been achieved. There are times when smaller goals are needed in order to sustain the large-scale goal that has already been accomplished. Life is a journey, not a destination. You never arrive, and as you journey through life, you will find that you acquire wisdom, knowledge, and life-lessons on the journey. Nothing is taught at the destination. The lessons are learned on the journey. Conceivably, most of your short-term goals are long-term goals broken up into chunks. For example, your long-term (four-year) goal could be to graduate from college with a bachelor's degree, but you may have a short-term (four-month) goal of completing five classes or 15 credits a semester. It is perfectly appropriate to have both long-term and short-term goals. In fact, it is recommended to have six months, one year, five years and also ten year goals. Time flies so fast and before you know it, ten years will be here, so why not prepare for it now?

Big Goals

The achievement of big goals gives the most gratification because they require the most sacrifice, effort, and hard work. Keep in mind that "big" to one person may be different from "big" to another person, so when the term big is used, it refers to what is big to you. When planning out your life, comparing your accomplishments to someone else's is a remedy for failure and discouragement, or it can contribute to feelings of superiority and preeminence. Comparing and competing with others is a big no no. The only one you should be competing with is yourself when it comes to goal attainment. The bigger your goals, the more sacrifice you must make. Big goals often come with the most obstacles and temporary setbacks, but those obstacles and temporary setbacks come with the territory of striving for massive success. No great goal was ever achieved easily. There must be a story in order to get the glory. The size of your belief determines the size of your accomplishments, so how big is your vision? The only limit there is on the size of your vision is the limit you place on yourself. The limit is where you draw the line. The sky should be the limit when it comes to how big your vision is.

Realistic Goals

It is great to have big goals, but are your goals realistic? To have a goal of acquiring a million dollars in a year is wonderful, but without realistic, attainable action plans to accomplish a million dollars, how are you going to acquire it? Writing goals down is powerful, but not *that* powerful. It's one thing to write goals down, but it's quite another to use the powers of your mind to create the action plans needed for manifestation of those goals. Goals should be challenging, but they must also be practical. They must be within your ability to reach. For example, I would not set a goal to win an academy award when I am not even an actress (being a drama queen doesn't count unfortunately).

Responsibility vs Accountability

Once you have developed your goals, it is expected that you will be responsible when striving to accomplish them. You have already demonstrated a great deal of commitment after you have written your personal affirmation/mission statement, developed your goals, then identified the actions steps needed to accomplish them, but that accountability piece is extremely critical. To whom are you going to be accountable besides yourself? Do you have enough self-discipline to light a fire under your butt when you have been slacking in pursuing your goals? More than likely, the answer is no. You need an accountability partner. This is someone who is just as interested in your success as you are, and they are willing to put in as much time writing their personal affirmation and setting their own goals as you have. This person must question you when you are slacking, ask for due dates and hold you accountable for doing what you said you would do in the timeframe that you said you would do it.

Your Mastermind Alliance

Accountability is where your mastermind alliance comes in. A Mastermind Alliance consists of a group of people with like minds and spirits who are just as committed to becoming as successful as you are. Everyone in the Mastermind Alliance develops goals and action plans for themselves. There are also goals for the Mastermind Group as a whole. Meetings are held on a frequent and consistent basis and in the meetings, individual reports are read on the progress of goals that members in the group have made. A report is given from each person in some or all of the nine areas (spiritual, financial, educational, family, recreational, personal, health, business/career, and community service). It is vital that everyone in the group is in harmony with one another because in the meetings, aspirations and personal goals are divulged, plans for accomplishing them are delineated, and guidance from members in the group is sought and given. Aspirations are discussed in detail and direction and advice is given. Sometimes constructive criticism is given in order to steer you in the right direction. This criticism is necessary and must be given in the right spirit. Oftentimes constructive criticism can save us from years of wasted time. Even in life, criticism is sometimes needed in order to make us, or our ideas better. We must be open to constructive criticism when it is valuable and beneficial. The ego may be bruised for a minute, but gratitude will eventually emerge as we see that our best interest was the objective when the criticism was conveyed. The trouble with most of us is that we would rather be ruined by praise than saved by criticism. The Mastermind Meetings must be beneficial, productive, encouraging, inspiring, and serious in nature. In an effective Mastermind Group, everyone benefits from the knowledge, education, and experience of everyone else. Your aspirations are not to be broadcasted to the world before they come into fruition. They are to be revealed to your Mastermind Group and perhaps your closest loved ones. The best way to show the world what you are going to do, is to show the world what you have already done. The Mastermind principle holds the secret to power. This principle is practiced by massively successful people who surround themselves with other people with great minds. No one person has sufficient experience, education, and knowledge to make it in this world without the cooperation of other people. Every plan you adopt in your endeavor to accomplish your goals should be the joint effort of yourself and other members of your Mastermind Group. A group of minds allied together in a spirit of harmony will provide more thought energy and power than a single mind alone. You must illustrate what you know. Talk is cheap. You must demonstrate your worth. You only accomplish as much as you can prove by manifestation. The credibility of your word is in your accomplishments.

     A study of rich and powerful men and women throughout the ages would reveal their frequent association with their Mastermind Alliance. Records reveal that Andrew Carnegie, Henry Ford, Oprah Winfrey, Barack Obama, Larry Page, Mark Zuckerburg, Warren Buffett, and many other prominent and powerful individuals had or continue to have a Mastermind Group that they meet with on a frequent basis. Powerful organizations, corporations and all types of companies have Boards of Directors, Advisory Boards, or Executive Teams, which is nothing but a Mastermind Group that meets to discuss the progress and future development of the entity. No man is an island. You need people in order to help get you where you desire to go. The key is to be able to identify trustworthy, reliable people who share similar ideologies and who are as serious about making an impact in this world as you are. If you are not a part of a Mastermind Group, then form your own.

Maximize Each Day

     The successful days get you where you want to go. If every day is unproductive, you will never achieve your goals, but if every day is a success, then you will not fail to achieve what you desire. You should be doing something daily with your goals that will bring you closer to their accomplishment. Time waits for no one and time will pass you by unless you make sufficient use of it. Money may buy you many things, but it cannot buy you more time. Everybody is given the same 24 hours in a day. The same amount of time is available in equal amounts to everyone whether you are rich or poor, man or woman, Black or White, educated or un-educated. Wealthy people do not get 36 hours in a day while poor people only get 24 hours. We all get equal amounts of time - 24 hours a day, seven days a week, 365 days a year. What you do with your time is what makes the difference. Continuous development and meaningful growth happens when you make the proper use of your 24 hours. If you are a failure today, it is because of your inappropriate use of past time. If you are a success today, it is because of your effective use of past time. If you can and will make the right use of your time, you will become a success. Sometimes you have to give up sleep and entertainment at the present in order to get you where you want to be in the future. Work hard and sacrifice while you are young, so that you can relax and take it easy when you are old. When you relax and take it easy when you are young, then you must unfortunately work hard and sacrifice when you are old. It is true that all work and no play makes Jack a dull boy, but all play and no work makes Jack a poor boy. Jack needs a balanced amount of both. The things you do in each of your 24 hours must be performed in an efficient manner. Not many things indifferently, but one thing supremely is the demand of this world. If you scatter your efforts, you will never succeed. If you do things in a half-finished, insufficient manner, you will not succeed either. You have the tools inside you to succeed through goal-setting and action planning. Now it's time to get to work!

Success Keys

* You have everything you need inside of you to accomplish your goals. The only thing that can stop you from pursuing your goals is YOU!

* Properly setting goals can be incredibly motivating. As you get into the habit of setting and achieving goals, you will find that your self-confidence increases quickly. This is a sure way to increase self-esteem.

* The majority of people meet with failure because of their lack of persistence in creating new plans to take the place of the ones that have failed. When they don't see instant results, they become discouraged and quit. There will be some failure, but that is okay.

* The elevator to success is broken. You must take the stairs. In all human affairs there are efforts and there are results, and the strength of the effort is the measure of the result.

* Sometimes you have to give up sleep and entertainment at the present in order to get you where you want to be in the future.

5
The Foundation of Success

A successful man is one who can lay a firm foundation with the bricks others have thrown at him.
~David Brinkley

Many spend countless days and sometimes years dreaming about success, but never put forth the necessary effort to do anything concrete to acquire it. It is the inherent aspiration of most people to live abundantly and to rise above the rut of living in lack, limitation, and from paycheck to paycheck. The majority of people equate success with money, but money is simply a tool used to buy things that we want to possess. The outgrowth of success and prosperity is not only identified in dollars and cents, but is also seen in terms of health. Good health is wealth. Financial wealth is typically a signal that one has applied the laws of success, but having money does not necessarily mean that one is successful. A person could have inherited millions of dollars, but still have a poverty consciousness. With a poverty consciousness, money will not last for long. Although people may have money and the symbols that indicate money (luxurious houses, classy cars, fine clothes, eating in fancy restaurants, expensive jewelry, etc.), that does not mean that they are successful or prosperous. To most people viewing from the outside, it would certainly mean that, but what they think they see could very well not be what it appears to be. Too many strive extremely hard to put up facades in order to maintain the appearance of prosperity when in actuality they are struggling financially, struggling psychologically and sometimes struggling mentally because they do not have a solid success consciousness. Success is a mindset. Once the mind has been permeated in the solid understanding of the laws of success, the embodiment of that revelation is manifested in the outward life. For those who are not content with living in mediocrity, there are success principles that must be followed and will work if implemented. Certain laws that pertain to success and prosperity are immutable, and must be adhered to on the part of the one seeking. Success is connected to spiritual principles, and it is essential to understand what those principles are, so that you will not be ignorant as to why struggle occurs.

Fulfillment

Fulfillment in life is becoming what you desire to be, and you can only become what you desire to be by making effective use of the responsibilities over which you have now. Every role and responsibility you have, has been given to you to propel you to where you need to be. Take nothing lightly. When you see an old lady struggling to cross the street, help her. That opportunity has been designed just for you. How will you handle it? Will you ignore her and keep going your way because you are in a rush, or will you help her? Every situation we encounter has been presented to us in order to push us forward. How we respond to each situation determines if we are to advance to the next level. As you cultivate and enhance what you have been given, you will prove yourself worthy of being elevated to more. It is therefore critical that you enhance and embrace the situations that are presented to you. The things that you may enhance may include your skills, your talents, your money, your position on the job, your marriage, your children, etc. Being a good steward over the things you have been given, will prove you worthy of receiving more. Most people usually focus on wanting more money, but when all other things line up, more money will come. You must look at all aspects of your life to determine if you have been faithful. If you have not been faithful over minor areas, how can you be faithful with money, which is an even greater responsibility?

Money

For centuries, people without money have turned their noses up at the rich, as though being rich was a terrible sin. To some degree today, people still embrace that mentality towards the rich, even though in their own heart of hearts, they wish they themselves were rich. You are in a much better position to help others with money than without it. You can do more good for the world with money than you can without it. Who doesn't desire to have enough money to afford what their hearts desire? Who does not dream of being rich? The majority of people do dream of it, but only a small percentage pursue it. You have a right to be rich, but you will not be entrusted with thousands of dollars if you are not faithful with the hundreds you have; and you will not be entrusted with hundreds of thousands of dollars if you have not been faithful with the thousands. You definitely will not be entrusted with millions if you have not been faithful with the hundreds of thousands. Many are asking for more when they have not been faithful over what they already have. They do not need more, they simply need to be better stewards over what they already have. Only with money can we be free and unrestricted to have the things that are necessary to reach our highest potential; but we must prove ourselves worthy of being able to handle large quantities of money. Regardless of what people say, not having money to pay bills and having to worry if the electricity, water, or telephone is going to be turned off does not produce peace, it produces worry. Not having money for food, clothes, or shoes for the children is not a good state of mind to be in. How can one be at peace if their basic needs are not met? How can one be at peace if their child has worn-out shoes too small for them, but there is no money to buy another pair? Worrying and peace do not cohabitate. If you have worry, you cannot have peace. Lack and limitation produces worry. Money brings some degree of peace and comfort. It is frustrating not having enough money to meet your needs. I have been there. I know what it's like. When you don't have enough money to buy basic necessities, you cannot adequately fulfill, nor live up to your full potential because worry clouds your peace of mind and you cannot focus and have clarity of thought. How can one focus on pursuing their dreams when their stomach is growling for food or their baby needs milk, or their home is in foreclosure? People constantly say that you do not need money to succeed, but that is not completely true. Money is needed in your pursuit for success. You may not need a large amount at first, but you will need a sufficient amount along the way. When you have made up in your mind to succeed, and you have put steps in place to reach your dreams, you send out a message to the universe telling it that you have positioned yourself to bring your dreams into fruition. Your magnetism draws to you the elements needed to bring those dreams into reality. There are specific laws associated with acquiring money and if learned, obeyed, and practiced, will magnetize avalanches of money to you. Not having money should never stop you from developing and writing your goals or dreams down. It should not stop you from identifying action steps, making a business plan, or doing research. You should do those things because when you do, you are sending out the message that you are preparing to receive what you do not yet have, but your action steps pave the way for their fruition.

Room for one More

The wealthy have certain patterns of thinking that draws money to them. Their minds are a magnet for money because they have the money consciousness. If people in your inner circle, your town, your city, your state and your country can become rich, then so can you! Regardless of what your bank account may look like today, if you begin doing certain things in a deliberate and strategic way, and cultivating certain thought patterns, you will begin to draw money to you. Ask largely. Expect to receive big. There are no limitations. The only limit there is, is the limit that you put on what you believe you can receive. No one is deprived because an opportunity passed them by or because someone stopped them from pursuing their heart's desire, or because there is not enough room for another rich person, or because they came from a poor family, etc. There are many excuses that you can use, but no one is going to feel sorry for you. Excuses won't bring success to you. You must get out there, roll up your sleeves and work. You can achieve success if you have a strong desire and dogged tenacity to do so. There is *always* room for one more, but you must compel that room for yourself. Just as a seed multiples after being planted, life by living multiplies itself also. Plant your seeds and watch them multiply. The desire for more money is really the desire to have greater fulfillment in life. Never look at what seems to be a lack or shortage in the natural, instead,

> *Excuses won't bring success to you. You must get out there, roll up your sleeves and work.*

fix your spiritual eye on the unlimited supply in divinity. Looking at things in the natural produces bondage, not freedom. Look at things as they can be, or better yet, as they will be.

It is of extreme importance not to make the mistake of thinking that money is the key that will solve all of your problems, because that is a great deception. Money may get you out of debt and may enable you to buy many nice things, but money is not the cure all. Although money can pay for an image consultant, it does not cure a defected personality. Although money can pay for medical research, money cannot eradicate a terminal disease. Although money may be used for good, it does not turn evil into good. In fact, it sometimes makes people more evil. Money may buy you a beautiful mansion of spectacular magnificence, filled with priceless works of art and breathtaking awnings, and it can fill your house with extravagant furniture, your garage with classic automobiles, but money cannot buy you a home filled with love and respect from the people who live there. Money can buy you the greatest doctors with the greatest minds in your hour of sickness, but money cannot buy you the God-given gift of health. Money can buy you lots of food, but money cannot buy you a healthy appetite. Money can buy a church pew with your name engraved on it in platinum, but money cannot buy you a ticket to heaven. Money will attract people to you like bees to honey, but money cannot buy you the treasure of one true friend. Money can buy you a bed of solid gold, but money cannot buy you one minute of rest or inner peace. Money can buy a crucifix around your neck, but money cannot buy a savior in your heart. Do not be deceived, money can do lots of good, but as you can see, there is much that money cannot do. It cannot buy you inner healing and peace of mind. Do not let money be your sole focus. Enjoy the journey. Stay grounded. Be a good steward and use your money wisely, but do not let money be the only thing you seek. Seek lessons. Seek to serve. Seek wisdom. Seek peace.

Success Principles

Prosperity is directly linked to strategic actions and patterns of thinking, but positive thinking must be supplemented with action. Goals must be supplemented with action! Vision must be supplemented with action! These actions and patterns of thinking must be consistently performed out of habit and self-discipline. At different seasons, the tide of opportunity sets in different directions according to the needs of the whole. When the tides advance, there is prosperity; when they recede, there is recession. However, if the laws and principles of prosperity are still being implemented in your life, then the advancing and receding of the tides will not affect your success since success is a mindset. On the next few pages, you will find a list of principles to which success is linked. When strategically applied to your life, these principles will not fail to prove infallible.

Success Principle #1: Monitor Your Mindset

Your success is linked to your mindset. Although the power of the mind was discussed in great detail in chapter one, it is beneficial to reiterate the importance of mastering your mind. To reverse your fortune is to reverse your thinking. Your life is shaped by the thoughts you think. Your thoughts attract people, circumstances and events to you. You act according to what you are thinking. Your actions and your thinking are always in harmony with each other. Therefore, if you are thinking positive, happy, prosperous thoughts, your behavior will be pleasant, happy and joyful. Things and people that make up your exact thought elements will be drawn to you because like attracts like. On the contrary, if your thoughts are negative, self-deprecating, and focused upon the worse, then your behavior will be negative, unpleasant, and self-deprecating. The situation will become bigger because you are sending out the thought magnet that will draw elements of the same nature of thoughts that you are thinking. Your mind must be trained to dismiss anything that enters it that you do not wish to see manifested. A prosperous mind focuses upon all that is good, affluent, fruit bearing, and peaceful regardless of what things look like from the natural perspective. A prosperous mind is optimistic, positive, confident, and always hopeful. This mind travels the road to success and understands that poverty and prosperity travel in two distinctly opposite directions. Although one's environment may seem grim and depressing, their mind can live in the environment of beauty and affluence. In time, their body will carry them to where their mind is because where the mind goes, the body will follow.

  Connecting yourself with people on a higher mental, intellectual, financial, and/or spiritual level will help to expand your mindset and raise you up to the level they are. As you resonate upon their success acumen, you will begin to focus upon those things as well. Successful people talk about ideas, plans, how to increase their business, how to positively brand themselves, how to make business connections, how to serve, etc. They do not have time for gossiping, complaining, or feeling sorry for themselves. There is no room for that in their consciousness. Their mindsets are expanded to receive big things. They realize that they cannot get to the millionaire level with a hundred dollar mindset. There is a great benefit in sitting under the tutelage of the great. If you currently have millionaires as friends, it's because you are on your way to becoming one. The people you hang around will help to expand your mindset - or shrink it down to their size. A prosperous mind is a guarded mind. This mind always has a watchman at the gate ready to turn away negativity and worry. If a negative thought happens to sneak in, a prosperous mind will detect it and evict it immediately. A prosperous mind is a strong mind that attracts and magnetizes all that is good, and these good thoughts are reflected in the personality and outward life. We are only given one life and when we begin to realize that our thoughts, imaginations, and meditations shape our lives and circumstances, we will be very careful of what we entertain when thinking. You are where you are because your thinking has brought you there. Where will your thoughts of today take you tomorrow? Be positive. Think positive. Act positive. Your mind creates your circumstances.

Success Principle #2: Your Meditation is your Medication

Your success is linked to your meditation. Meditation brings about revelation. Meditation is essential when it comes to giving life to your highest dreams. It gives life to your visions. A vision can be broad at first, but an imagination makes it detailed and meditation gives it form and life. When you become proficient in meditation, you will begin to feel the embodiment of the things meditated upon. No one ever receives anything good in life unless they first *imagine* it and *feel* it. When you begin to feel it, the focus has been transferred from your conscious mind to your subconscious mind and from there it is just a matter of time before the ideal becomes the real.

Your outcome will not change until your focus changes. Meditation is the chief way to become successful in every area of your life. Change will not happen until you get an image of something new. In order to change your life, change what you picture in your mind. Change your imagination. What you focus on the longest becomes the strongest. You have in your life right now everything that you focused on long enough. If you are constantly facing the same problem, it is because you have not changed your focus. What are you constantly focusing on? When you focus on it long enough, it becomes meditation. Demand inwardly that a change in your life will happen. When you do that, you will begin to imagine a totally different world, one that reflects the express image of how you desire things to be from your inward perspective. Then, meditate upon that. Every great leader uses his or her imagination in order to create something out of a realm that is void of form. Imagination gives the blueprint and meditation gives the form.

Whatever you cannot see, you cannot have. If you cannot see it, you will not receive it. If you do not believe it, you will not achieve it. The most powerful forces in the world are invisible: electricity, wind, radio waves, etc. Your most powerful forces are invisible too: your thoughts, meditations, imaginations, love, ambition, perseverance, etc. These forces are silent, unseen and unfelt. But when you tap into the power that you already have and activate that power through meditation, it takes you to great heights of achievement. Everything you need is already within you. You must go within. Meditation upon your success is a daily practice, a lifestyle. Do it until it becomes a part of you. In order to get something new, you must think something new, imagine something new, and meditate on something new. When you begin to meditate, you become focused on higher purposes. It is in meditation that you truly find out who you are. You come face to face with the real you.

You must be strategic with your meditation time. It must be designated. If you meditate on your aspirations at the wrong times, you steal energy and focus that needs to be put towards what you should be doing in the present. You cannot work in a spirit of excellence with a divided mind. You cannot effectively perform in the present with your mind on the future. In order to rise from mediocre to good and from good to great, you must do things in a spirit of excellence at all times. For this reason, time should be designated for meditation on the ideal, but the duties of the current day must be fulfilled in a spirit of excellence in that day.

Success Principle #3: Establish & Maintain Your Brand
Successful people develop and maintain their brand because they realize that their brand carries much weight. Your brand can make or break you personally or professionally. Branding is creating an image in the minds of people about the quality of your product and the benefits it has to others. Branding is also creating an image in the minds of people about who *you* are and what *you* do. Branding automatically connects you with something. A good personal brand is created when people hear your name and your product and immediately connect you with what you do or what your product is. When people associate you with EXACTLY what you want them to, then your branding is effective. A good personal brand is created when your subject area is brought up in conversation and YOUR NAME comes up. Effective Personal Branding opens doors for you, but good service keeps those doors open!

A brand does not necessarily say, "buy me" or "buy my product", it says, *This is what I am. This is why I exist. If you like me or my product, you can buy me, support me, and recommend me to your friends.* Your brand conveys that message without spoken words. Of course, once others buy into your brand, you must deliver. If you have a good brand, you must have the good service to back up all the hype. Successful people realize this and make both their brand and their service high quality.

Success Principle #4: Giving Brings Great Returns

Your success is linked to your giving. Every time you give, you are sowing a seed. When you are blessed, you must bless others. Everyone was born with two hands for a reason, one hand to give, and the other to receive. There must be a constant inflow and outgoing. You will never hold on to anything for long if you hoard them. If you tied a rope around your leg, circulation would be cut off after a while and your leg would die. It is the same with things. If there is no circulation, there is no flow. There must be a back and forth flow of going out and coming back in. The world operates on the principle of giving and receiving. Wherever there is an obstruction, there is greed. There can be no one-way flow. The mysterious part about giving is that the seed you sow never leaves your life. It only leaves your hand temporarily then goes into your future where it multiplies and awaits your arrival. Never give with the expectation of being paid back. You are repaid in *due season*. Prosperous people sow seeds and they give generously!

Success Principle #5: Your Friends are a Mirror of You

Your success is linked to your friends and associations. You must be watchful of the people you choose to spend time with and allow into your inner circle. Your associations can help or hinder you. They will either enhance or decease your image and credibility.

Bad associations will corrupt a good character. Take an inventory of who is around you. People come into your life to add, subtract, multiply, or divide. Are your friends adding to your life or subtracting? multiplying? or dividing? Review those in your life to make sure they are adding to you as a person, not subtracting from your strength and vigor. The wrong people will hold you back, bring you drama, drag you down, and drain you of your creative energy. You can only move forward with the right people in your inner circle. Acquaint yourself with people who have already achieved what you are trying to achieve. If you hang with eagles, you will learn to fly high. Do you ever see black birds mixing with white birds? How about eagles with jay birds? What about chickens with pigeons? How about ducks and roosters hanging out together? Whenever you see birds conjugating, they are always of the same feather; so it is with humans. We conjugate with those we are like. Thieves hang with thieves, politicians hang with politicians, educators hang with educators, etc. Like attracts like in everything. Great people hang around great people, do great things, and exude great confidence. You become like those you interact with the most. Those who do not increase you will eventually decrease you. It is better to be alone than in the wrong company. You are wise when you learn and practice this truth. Some of your friends and acquaintances are fine for where you are now, but not for where you are going. In order to gain some things, you must give up some things, and nonproductive people may be something to give up. The space left behind by them will be filled with a new caliber of people who will propel you to the next level of success.

> *The wrong people will hold you back, bring you drama, drag you down, and drain you of your creative energy. You can only move forward with the right people in your inner circle.*

Success Principle #6: Conversations Bring Manifestations

Your success is linked to your conversations. You attract what you talk about. This universe is run by conversations between people. You may just be one conversation away from your massive success, but if you are too high and mighty to hold a conversation with someone you feel is beneath you, you may just miss out on a blessing. You cannot work hard enough for what you want on your own. At some point, you will need favor, and you may never know who that favor will come through. It could be the person you least expect. When you change the nature of your conversations, you change your conditions, your mindset, and your reality. The more specific you are when speaking, the more powerful your results will be. Powerful statements produce powerful results.

There is power in your words that go out into the universe and attracts the elements that are needed in order for success to come into fruition. The words used in your conversations do return to you for better or for worse. Who you are and what you think or feel is always revealed in your conversations. No one knows the quality of your mind until you open your mouth and speak. Your daily conversations reveal what you think about, what you believe in, what you agree with and attract certain things and people to you. Your life is shaped by the words you speak. Be strategic in your conversations. Use affirmative words and eradicate negative, self-defeating words out of your conversations. Exude positive energy, light, encouragement, confidence and optimism in your conversations with people.

Success Principle #7: An Attitude of Gratitude

Your success is linked to your gratitude. Gratitude unlocks the door to the fullness of life. It turns what you have into more than enough. Gratitude turns rejection into acceptance, chaos into order, and confusion into clarity. It can turn a meal into a feast, a house into a home, and a stranger into a friend. Gratitude makes sense of your past and brings peace for today, while creating a vision for tomorrow. When you give thanks for what you already have, you open a floodgate of blessings that begin moving in your direction. Gratitude places you on a current that draws more your way. There is always something for which to be grateful. I once read the following quote stated by Buddha, which sums up for me that there is always something to be grateful for: *"Let us rise up and be thankful, for if we did not learn a lot today, at least we learned a little, and if we did not learn a little, at least we didn't get sick, and if we got sick, at least we did not die, so let us still be thankful."* Begin to feel the spirit of gratitude now. Be grateful for your many blessings. Your strong thankful emotion will draw more to be thankful for. Be grateful for the good times and the bad, the rain and the sunshine, the victories and the defeats, the joys and the sorrows, because all of them teach lessons.

Success Principle #8: Actions Speak Louder Than Words

Your success is linked to your efficient and productive actions. Regardless of how much faith you have and how earnestly you have put all of the other principles to work in your life, if there is no action on your part, then everything else is in vain. No matter how positive you think, you must also roll up your sleeves and get to work! Your thoughts and actions must be in harmony. You must "do" something every day that will bring you closer to the vision that you are holding in your mind. By thought, the image of what you want is given to you, but by *action* it is received. Hold the vision of your future aspirations before you always until they manifest, but act always in the present. You must know how to compartmentalize well. Meditate on what you desire to have, but work with excellence on what you already have. Make mental room for what is coming, but treat what is already there with gratitude. You can only be great by being larger than your presence space; but if you leave the work undone in your present space, then you are not larger than your present place. The progress of the world is stifled by those who do not complete the work in their present place. How can the world advance if everyone was smaller than their present space? It is the successful days that bring you into greatness. If your actions each day are successful, then you cannot fail to obtain success.

Your neglect or failure to complete a small action today could delay you in years of reaching your highest dream. You must first have a prosperity mindset. Set your goals, develop your plans, work hard, sacrifice, toil, labor, and then be patient. If you are not willing to do those things, then do not be envious of those who do and are experiencing the fruit of their hard work, labor, and sacrifice. Work is the therapy of the soul. God Himself worked six days in the creation of the heaven and earth. You can become quite successful without formal education, influential friends, or even significant seed capital, but you will never be successful with weak faith, lack of planning, and poor work habits. Success, prosperity, and wealth are not going to just appear into your life. You must put in the work!

Success Principle #9: *Never let your pen be idle.*

Writing down your goals, aspirations, dreams and desires makes them concrete. When you articulate your goals, your plans, your dreams and your desires out of your mouth, you make them more likely to happen, but when you write them out, you make them five times more likely to happen. Writing is the first step in bringing your intangible vision into three-dimensional manifested form. Writing serves as a power source and lasting impression that continues to exist even after you have stopped writing. When you write things down, you set things in motion because you have pulled the written word out of the mental realm into the physical realm. Writing serves as an entry point for the transition out of the invisible realm into the visible realm. Write down how much money you want to bring in each month, what you want to see happen in your marriage, on your job, in your household. Write down the ultimate dream career you desire to have, the places you want to travel. Write down what you want to see come to fruition in your future. When you write for your future, you are actually stepping into it and setting things in motion to wait for your arrival. Write down everything you desire to see manifested into your life. There is a great power in writing! Your vision will not be a success until you can believe in it enough to write it out and display it up on a billboard! Writing is thought that is given permanence. Your thoughts, tongue and hand must become the pen of a ready writer.

Success Principle #10: Recognition is Insight

Your success is linked to your awareness and ability to recognize. Too many have sight, but no vision. Too many have eyes, but cannot see. Learn to discern. The ability to recognize can raise you from the rut of mediocrity and place you on the mountain of greatness. Open your eyes and see! Recognition can mean the same thing as discernment or awareness. You must have vision to be able to recognize opportunities, money-making ideas, distractions, blessings, and quality people. Anything valuable in your life that you fail to recognize will not be celebrated. If it is not celebrated, it will not be rewarded, if it is not rewarded, then it will leave. We tend to look at people and sometimes wonder what "breaks" they had in life. We often fail to realize that most people make their own breaks when they place themselves in positions to receive them. Breaks often come when you recognize opportunities and take hold of them quickly. If you fail to recognize what is before you, you may miss out on a once-in-a-lifetime opportunity. Let's look at some important things to be recognized on the next few pages.

Recognition of Opportunities

The ability to recognize is a valuable asset. Opportunities come a dime a dozen, but there are some opportunities that have *your* name specifically stamped on them. Those are designed to be keys that will unlock more doors leading to even greater success. You must be able to discern which opportunity is worth pursuing and which is not. If you venture into every opportunity that comes your way, you will waste a lot of time and money. You will need an eagle's eye to know what to pursue and what not to pursue. One of the saddest things in the world is for someone not to be able to recognize a once-in-a-lifetime opportunity when it is presented to them, only to find out later that those who stayed for the long haul became millionaires. I have read the story of those who were part of the original group with Larry Page and Sergey Brin exploring the Google concept. There were some who could not see the vision and abandoned the idea. Others caught the vision, saw the potential in it and remained to help streamline the idea. Today Google is the number one internet search engine in the world. The company profited 37.9 billion dollars in revenue in 2011. As of this writing (August 2013), their stocks closed at $865.42 per share on both the New York Stock Exchange and NASDAQ. Those who could not see the vision in the beginning missed out on the immense financial reward in the end. Some people may start out with you in the beginning, but if it is not in the plan for them to remain, eventually they will eliminate themselves along the way. I also heard similar stories about Facebook and other powerful empires. When people want to leave, let them leave. Not everyone will be able to see the vision. Just make sure that you can. A once-in-a-lifetime opportunity is just that - once-in-a-lifetime.

Recognition of Money-making Ideas

Money comes from ideas. With implemented ideas, you can accomplish much more than the one limited thing you may be asking for. The principle is similar to the popular adage: *Give a man a fish and he will eat for a day, but teach him to fish and he will eat for a lifetime.* Open your mind to receive wealth-begetting ideas. Houses, cars and money are only byproducts of implementing the ideas that come to you. The blessing is the *idea* and the ability to bring life to it, not the house, the money, or the car.

Success, prosperity, and wealth are not going to just appear on your doorstep. Once you get an idea, you must plan the work and work the plan. Many people start things and never finish any of them. They have too many scattered projects. Great people finish what they start no matter how big or small the task is. When you begin to implement an idea, you must see it all the way through. That is the only way you will get the reward. *"If a task is once begun, never leave it til it's done; be the labor great or small, do it* well or not at all" (author unknown). Recognize money-making ideas, then finish what you start and you will feel a great sense of accomplishment.

Recognition of Quality people

If we judge people based upon their appearance only, we could miss an important message or great blessing that they may have for us. There are millionaires who look like beggars and there are those who look like millionaires, but barely have two nickels to rub together. Look past appearance and listen to the value and knowledge that a person may possess. They may have just what you need to help propel you higher.

Recognition of Distractions

People will call you with foolishness and try to get you caught up in their vain endeavors. Keep your mind and your focus prioritized. Having awareness and insight is the ability to be able to identify distractions. Gossip serves as a distraction. Intermingling in the business of others is a distraction. Focusing upon things that yield no positive fruit serves as a distraction. Even watching vain television shows can be a distraction. Recognize what distracts you and refocus yourself accordingly. Achieving success requires both mental and physical exertion. Anything worth having is worth working for and then waiting for. After exerting the time and energy towards the attainment of your goals and putting in the mental strength and necessary actions, you will find that all of your efforts will turn out to be far less than the reward received if you refuse to become distracted. The time, sacrifice, mental effort and appropriate actions are all seeds sown. When harvest arrives, you will find that the few seeds planted were multiplied, and gave you double for your trouble. You simply cannot afford to waste time on distractions when you could be sowing seeds.

The foundation of success must be laid solid and strong with success principles, focus, and good habits. If the foundation is weak, the success tower will fall. It is one thing to achieve success, but quite another to maintain it and be able to leave an inheritance for your children and their children. Keep in mind that the successful have different habits from the mediocre. They do things that the average do not like to do. The highly successful person goes over and beyond the bare minimum, they make sacrifices, they avoid distractions and they seek to serve. Lay your foundation with these success principles.

Success Keys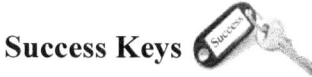

* Prosperity is a mindset and begins in the mind. Once the mind has been saturated in the understanding of the laws of prosperity, the embodiment of that revelation is manifested in the outward life.

* The wealthy have certain patterns of thinking that draws money to them. Their minds are a magnet for money because they have the money consciousness.

* At different seasons, the tide of opportunity sets in different directions according to the needs of the whole. When the tides advance, there is prosperity; when they recede, there is a recession.

* You are in a much better position to be able to help others with money than without it. You have a right to be rich, but you will not be entrusted with thousands of dollars if you have not been faithful with hundreds and you will not be entrusted with millions if you have not been faithful with thousands.

* Worrying and peace do not harmonize. If you have worry, you cannot have peace. Lack and limitation produces worry. Money brings some degree of peace and comfort.

6
Inner Healing

On the path to wellness one must learn to recognize fear. Particularly within ourselves. Anger is fear, jealousy is fear, even some ignorance. Health, however, is born from love.

~Author Unknown

We now understand that success entails more than just money and material possessions. Success is having peace in your mind, body, spirit *and* bank account. Being successful in one aspect of your life, but miserable in another is not being a true success. The goal is to have joy and peace as a result of being successful in all areas of your life. This may include success on your job, in your business, in your skills, your bank account, your marriage, your body, and in your soul. There are plenty of depressed and miserable millionaires in this world. Many people have reached their goals, but have no peace, no joy, no sense of accomplishment. What good does it do to be able to afford anything you want when you are unhappy, broken and miserable on the inside? There is no enjoyment of the fruit of your labor when you cannot find peace. The purpose of striving to be successful is to be able to bask in the feelings of self-gratification, joy, happiness, and tranquility that comes with having achieved success. When you have experienced a trauma or emotional scar that has not been dealt with, achieving success will not obliterate the pain, shame, guilt, anger or bitterness associated with the trauma.

For a while, those deep emotions may lie dormant, but eventually they will awaken, arise, and taunt you at night until you finally are forced to deal with them one way or another.

Emotional Baggage

History is what has happened in the past. Baggage is comprised of the emotions that resulted from negative experiences of the past that still lingers. Almost everyone has some measure of emotional baggage, but there are people who have way more than others to the degree that it affects their endeavors and relationships in almost every aspect of their lives. Baggage can cause fear, doubt, suspicion, mistrust, withdrawal, hesitation, or failure to love or be loved. Some people mask their pain by putting all of their energy and effort into obtaining success - and they do acquire it - but at the end of the day, they are still broken and hurting on the inside because their pain was never dealt with. They have secured financial gain, influence, respectability, and self-gratification from the achievement of their goals, but they still have a void and a wounded soul. These feelings are hidden behind a big wall that people put up to protect themselves. They carry this wall with them into each relationship they have. When emotional baggage runs deep, its effects can sabotage relationships or business dealings that would otherwise have long term potential. The tricky thing about emotional baggage is that most do not realize they are still carrying it around within them, even after it has revealed itself time and time again. When emotion from baggage emerges, it is disguised by a situation or issue that has arisen between you and someone else. The way in which the situation is dealt with and the things that are said and done while dealing with the issue determines if it's the baggage that has surfaced or not.

You must analyze whether your baggage has contributed to failure in past relationships and/or business endeavors. If so, then the time may have come to face those painful hurts of the past and deal with them appropriately if you are to move forward positively towards achieving success. Even if it has been years or even decades since the events occurred, it is never too late to get healed. If you notice that the same problems arise in all your relationships, then you must take a closer look at any negative emotions and fears to which you may be clinging. The only factor that all of your failed relationships have in common is you. Therefore, you know that the only way to stop the sabotaging patterns from presenting themselves in yet more relationships lies within you.

Baggage that Seeps out

We must learn how to recognize emotional baggage in order to enjoy healthy and happy relationships with people. When a hurt is experienced that is not resolved or dealt with appropriately, those unresolved feelings are then internalized, which causes mental anguish and emotional turmoil. The suppression adds to the layers of hurt that are already there. The pain seeps out sporadically because there has been no release or eradication of it. The baggage is therefore carried over into relationships, friendships, business dealings, meetings, etc. The same fears and negative emotions trigger irrational thoughts and unreasonable behaviors that contribute to the ultimate decline of whatever it is that you were involved in. This is a cycle from which you are unable to escape until the root causes of your hurt are dealt with. Until then, you will go from person to person and situation to situation thinking that if you find the "right" people things will be okay. After all, everyone else has a problem, not you. This is a delusion.

Women tend to have more emotional baggage than men, although there are many men who have experienced deep psychological hurt and traumatic pain just like women. Men are less inclined to talk about their issues, which creates a much deeper suppression contributing to deterioration in their relationships as well. People are walking around with deeply rooted issues, emotional scars, and intense pain everyday stemming from things that have happened in their childhood, teenage years, early adult years, adulthood, past relationships, and even stemming back from toddler age. They put on a smile and tuck their pain deep into the corners and crevices of their soul and keep it moving, all the while praying that no one can see what's on the inside. They do everything in their power to keep from having to revisit their past. Unless those issues are dealt with head on, they will never disappear, but will raise their ugly head making themselves known at the most inopportune times.

Strategies for Releasing Emotional Baggage

Emotional baggage can be caused by many different things including sexual molestation, rape, abandonment, rejection, physical, verbal or emotional abuse, heartbreaks, domestic violence, mistreatment, divorce, grief, being cheated on, etc. The causes of emotional baggage and hurt really are not the main issue, however. The main issue, which is the key to effective healing is how you deal with that baggage. When you choose to try and forget about the pain by not talking about it, and try to live life as though those horrible things never happened, you will never truly be free, nor can you ever be until those issues are dealt with. Facing your past changes your future in positive ways. Allow yourself to learn from those experiences.

Inner Healing

Below are some things that you can do to release your emotional baggage so that you can move forward and begin cultivating healthy relationships:

- Talk to someone about what happened to you. Explain how you felt then, how you feel now, and how you will move forward in the future in spite of it. A therapist, counselor, psychologist, priest, pastor, or someone that you trust can help with this. When you get it out by talking about it, you will feel better because you are beginning to release it. When you hold on to it and refuse to discuss it, you continue to feel weighted down with the burden of constantly carrying that baggage around in your soul.

- When facing the events that hurt you, allow yourself to "feel" the pain from those emotions and then deal with them appropriately: anger, sadness, fear, frustration, guilt, shame, rejection, sorrow etc. Coming to terms with your past is not easy, but it is necessary in order for you to move on.

- Forgive yourself and believe that in spite of what happened, you are still worthy of happiness, peace and joy.

- Forgive those who hurt you. It may not be easy, but the only way to move forward is to release them and forgive them.

- Allow yourself to acknowledge that your past does not determine your future. The past is gone. There is no changing it. Therefore, look forward to great things happening in your future because you deserve greatness. You cannot go forward if you are stuck in reverse. Don't let your history interfere with your destiny!

- Release all of the emotional hurt and fears that are weighing you down by speaking directly to them. Say, *"You will no longer cause me guilt, shame, or _____. I release all the bitterness and discouragement connected to my past and I move forward with joy and peace toward my future!"*

- Accept and embrace the new person that you are becoming and live each day with the expectation that you are worthy of happiness.

- Keep a journal and write your feelings down in the same way you would talk to a friend about it.

- Develop a personal mission statement (PMS) for yourself and recite this PMS every chance you get. This is an affirmation of who you aspire to be mentally, physically, spiritually, financially and psychologically. Every time you recite it with conviction and faith, it sinks into your conscious mind and passes over into your subconscious mind until you actually become the person you say you are. It works!

As you have learned, emotional baggage sabotages relationships and can inhibit your success. You are an evolving being and you are constantly progressing and becoming a new person. It is only through experiences that you become well-rounded and strong. Human nature causes us to desire love, affection, and validation. There is nothing wrong with giving your heart to a person and allowing a person to give you theirs, but there are no guarantees in love and love does not come with a warning disclaimer. Sometimes you win and sometimes you lose in love. When it doesn't work out, it is essential that you effectively deal with it, so that your future success will not be affected negatively by it. Falling in love is a glorious feeling. Falling out of love is a frustrating and sometimes uncomfortable feeling; and experiencing a broken heart is a devastating and painful emotion. Although each of those emotions feel differently, it is beneficial to have experienced them all because they each will contribute to making you a stronger person. You will be able to encourage and uplift someone who will cross your path one day. They may need the wisdom from your experiences. The key is to appropriately deal with your painful experiences. Do not let them pile up in your heart, mind, and soul becoming emotional baggage. Move forward with confidence and assurance that your friendships, family relationships, business dealings, or romantic life will be successful and healthy; and if they are not, it will not be because you sabotaged them.

Rejection

Being rejected sometimes lowers self-confidence. Being accepted increases self-confidence. Unless the experience is used to propel you, having been rejected in the past will prevent you from pursing your highest goals. Fear of rejection is an inhibitor and stops you from moving forward by making you wonder if you will be given a no. At some point in your journey to success, you will have to humbly ask for help. Some will willingly say yes and do what they can to help you achieve your goals, and others will say no. The "nos" do not feel good, but if you look at the "nos" as a step further to a yes, then the "nos" won't bother you as much. Getting rejected teaches you to be strong, so you can understand when you have to give a no to someone.

Men, women, and children want to have their love returned more than anything; but being rejected does not always have to do with you, and you should not allow your self-confidence to suffer because of it. You cannot control how another person responds to you. It could just be your season to experience what rejection feels like. The person who rejects you is sometimes just the unlikely vessel used to bring that particular emotion to you. The most important thing that you should know about rejection is not to allow it to take root in you. At some point, you will have to get up and say to yourself that although a person may not have wanted to be with you, there is someone out there who does. We all experience various emotions at different times in our lives. These emotions are necessary in order for us to be balanced, well-rounded humans. Happiness, joy, success, excitement, love, gratification, sadness, anger, frustration, discouragement, and rejection are the basic human emotions that people experience during their lifetime. Needless-to-say, the sadness, anger, frustration, and rejection do not feel good, but the happiness, love, success, excitement, and joy sure does. We must experience them all in order to be balanced. There is no reason to get upset with the person who you feel rejected you. They should not be condemned for feeling the way they feel about you or not feeling the way you think they should feel. If their feelings for you

> *Getting rejected simply means that who or what you were rejected by was not meant for you. Point blank!*

do not parallel your feelings for them, then obviously they were not the one for you. This is no reason to put up a wall and not allow yourself to open up to a worthy person again and be loved in the future. You must move in the confidence and assurance that your rejection will be replaced by full and complete acceptance from someone else who will love you unconditionally. When you do not look at things this way, it makes achieving success harder because you are keeping your walls up, which allows no one to get past a certain layer.

You will never obtain true success and wealth as long as you are still wounded and broken from past hurt. Wealth is health. If you have millions of dollars, but are still hurting and broken, then you are not wealthy. You may be rich, but you are not successful and you are not whole. Keep in mind that true success is obtaining peace in every area of your life. Money can buy lots of things, but it cannot buy a new heart or soul in the place of the wounded ones. It cannot buy happiness, nor can it buy peace. You must go within in order to obtain these things. Once your leftover baggage from the past has been released and you have moved on from it, you will find that obtaining success coupled with inner peace, joy and happiness is a beautiful thing.

The Power of Release

Finally getting rid of your heavy baggage is liberating and invigorating. Once you experience the freedom that comes with letting all your baggage go, you will kick yourself for not letting it go sooner. Baggage weighs you down, causes distrust of other people, suspicion, overreaction, makes you assume the worse, causes you to make irrational decisions and produces lots of emotionalism. Release does just what its names says, it releases unforgiveness, stress, anger, sadness, fear, frustration, guilt, shame, rejection, etc. It is important to understand that whenever something is lost, something else is gained, so in the place of what has been released, other things will come. Those things include, but are not limited to, forgiveness, love, joy, peace, freedom, laughter, clear-thinking, and confidence. You actually become a new person and are able to truly enjoy the success that you have worked so hard for. In your pursuit for success, keep in mind that success is both inner peace and outer fulfillment. When there is peace on the inside, there will be peace and joy on the outside. True success is manifested in your life is only a mirror of the true peace and healing that has permeated on the inside. Seek success from within, then it will exude without. You have the inner strength to do it. When you seek it, you will find it.

Success Keys

* We must learn how to recognize emotional baggage in order to enjoy healthy and happy relationships with people. When a hurt is experienced that is not resolved or dealt with appropriately, those unresolved feelings are then internalized, which causes mental anguish and emotional turmoil.

* Emotional baggage sabotages relationships and can inhibit your success. You are an evolving being and you are constantly progressing and becoming a new person.

* Being rejected lowers self-confidence. Being accepted increases self-confidence. If not used to propel you forward,

having been rejected in the past will prevent you from pursing your highest goals.

★ You will never obtain true success and wealth as long as you are still wounded and broken from past hurt. Wealth is health. If you have millions of dollars, but are still hurting and broken, then you are not wealthy.

7
From Good to Great

Great minds discuss ideas; average minds discuss events;
small minds discuss people.
                              ~Eleanor Roosevelt

You may be great within, but the world must see that you are great without. There is a reason why there are many different kinds of people from many different backgrounds in this world. There are rich, poor, good, evil, sick, healthy, different races, above-average, mediocre, hard-working and downright slothful. From a theoretical standpoint, there needs to be a balance of elements in order to even out the earth. The majority of people in this world choose to be who and what they are. As we choose to be who we are, we invariably place ourselves in one of the aforementioned categories. We make our decisions either by hard work and determination or failure to go over and beyond the bare minimum. In all human affairs, there are efforts and there are results, and the strength put into the effort is the measure of the result. In America, we are all born free, but we are not all born equal; therefore, we each have different perceptions of failure and success. There is no reason why a person of average intellect and good health living in the United States should be poor as an adult, unless they choose to be so. It is one thing to be born poor, but quite another to live poor and die poor. We may not all be born rich, but we may acquire riches through the creative use of our minds.

America is referred to as the land of the free, the home of the brave. We are free to become whatever we want to become in America. Stop looking at where you have been and start looking at where you are going. The greatest days of your life are before you. In addition to the success principles delineated in chapter five, there are other habits and actions that success-minded people do, which enhances their success mindset and helps to maintain their success:

The Success-minded take risks.

Being elevated from good to great often requires risk-taking, which plays a big part of achieving the vision of success. Everyone at some point in their lives will take risks. Some risks are unavoidable but inevitable; others are voluntary and are just that - risks. Contrary to what has been told or taught, not all risks are bad. Some are well thought-out and intelligent. Others are foolish and unintelligent, but since I am writing for those who aspire to achieve success by utilizing the intelligent creativity of their minds, then I am focusing on intelligent risks. With intelligent risks, you consider the consequences, costs, pros, cons, advantages and disadvantages. The common phrase, *"Do not put all your eggs into one basket"*, means that you do not put everything on the line for the sake of a risk, even if it *is* an intelligent risk. A risk is still a risk, meaning that there is some possibility of loss, injury, or damage. Most average people do not like taking risks because it is out of their comfort zone. They find it much easier to settle for the status quo. It is easier to play it safe in all aspects of their lives. They keep their mouths closed, their money safe, and remain within the confines of their comfort zone; but sometimes in order to achieve massive success, you must take massive risks.

As with all things, your perception determines how bad a situation truly is. When we learn the art of comparing things to how bad it can really be, then our perspective of those things will shrink to their proper size. Instead of looking at a risk from a negative perspective, we can view it from a positive standpoint. In other words, we can look at a risk as the chance of winning big, of getting additional assets, of acquiring more, etc. These are the kinds of risks where the upside outweighs the downside, at least probability-wise. There are times in each person's life where a once-in-a-lifetime opportunity will come and it will require a quick decision and some risk-taking. What will you do? Just as it is not wise and sometimes downright foolish to take an unintelligent risk, it is equally as foolish to pass up an intelligent one, where your expected outcome is positive and the potential downside is limited. It does bear repeating: *The most intelligent risks are those where the potential downside is limited, but the potential upside is virtually unlimited.* Almost everything we do in life is a risk in some way, but we must do them anyway. In his book, 'The Seven Secrets' Author, founder and senior pastor of Cornerstone Church in San Antonio, Texas, a non-denominational mega church with more than 20,000 active members. John Hagee writes: *"Success will win you false friends and true enemies. Succeed anyway. The good you do today will be forgotten tomorrow. Do good anyway. The biggest people with biggest ideas can be shot down by mental midgets with the smallest ideas. Think big anyway. What you spend years building may be destroyed overnight, build anyway. People need help, but may attack you for offering your hand. Help them anyway."* For some risks taken, we will lose, but most we win, but without taking risks, we will never know.

The Success-minded work in a spirit of excellence.

Having a spirit of excellence is taking pride in what you do and making sure that it is done effectively. In essence, what you do is simply "exceptional." Going from good to great means having an excellent work ethic. Being excellent is what stands you out among the rest and makes you unique. While the average person has done the bare minimum, the person who has a spirit of excellence has done not only the minimum, but has gone far beyond that and much more. Even after they have surpassed the bare minimum, they go back and check their work to ensure that there are minimal to no errors. A spirit of excellence compels one to take pride in what they do. When they put their hands to something, their work is carried out in the most efficient and detail-oriented manner. The effectiveness with which they do things also carries over into their personal lives. People with this character trait often are meticulous in every area of their lives. Their effectiveness becomes part of their character which reaps great benefits. Many people start things, but never see them through until completion, but the person who has an excellent spirit, not only starts and finishes, but they finish big. Their end result is splendid and their excellent touch makes their work of superb quality.

The Success-minded follow through on what they start.

Without follow-through, you will never accomplish anything meaningful. Going from good to great will require frequent follow-through on a variety of things. Many people start worthy endeavors that, if they were to follow-through to the very end would bring enormous rewards; but unfortunately, they do not finish what they have started, so they never know what the end would have been. When you start something, but do not follow through until its completion, you have formed the habit of failure and your subconscious mind gets into the habit of not allowing you to complete anything. There are those who have attended college, taken a break, never went back, and then say they only need three or four more classes towards their college degree. No one cares about that. All people know is that they do NOT have a college degree. I personally know several people who started the commendable goal of obtaining their doctorate degree. They took all the classes, but never wrote the dissertation. Why pay all of that money, finish all of those classes, and never write the research paper? The task seems too big, that's why! Big things are only small things broken up into small chunks, but one would never know that if they didn't follow-through on anything. How many people do you know who started reading a book and never finished it? I hope you finish the one you are reading right now! If you feel that I am talking about you as I discuss starting projects and not finishing them, then let this book be the first one that you finish, and then email me when you do (merrittmia@yahoo.com). There is nothing worse than starting multiple tasks and not finishing any of them. When you start things and do not finish them, then at the end of the day what has really been accomplished? Nothing! All there is to show for your efforts are a bunch of incomplete projects. Make sure that you follow-through on every task you start until each task is completed.

> *When you start things and do not finish them, then at the end of the day, what has really been accomplished? Nothing! All there is to show for your efforts are a bunch of incomplete projects.*

The Success-minded make sacrifices.
Making sacrifices is something that all successful people have done in order to get where they are. When you have a strong desire to achieve massive success, you are focused, committed, and willing to make the necessary sacrifices in order to reach your desired goal.

Successful people do the things that average people do not like to do. They make sacrifices. They postpone the love of ease and pleasure for a while, realizing that while they have a main goal, the time and energy spent towards certain pleasures must be channeled towards their desired end. There are four main areas in which successful people often make sacrifices. They realize that they must at some point give these areas up in order to accomplish their goal of achieving success. These sacrifices are deliberately made by choice, and they are: 1. time 2. money 3. pleasure and 4. friendships.

The success-minded manage their time well.
Successful people know how to manage their time. They realize that money can buy lots of things, but it cannot buy more time. Successful people are not just busy, they are productive. They are well aware that what they do each day will bring rewards to them down the line. They understand that in order to eat the fruit of tomorrow's tree, they must plant the seeds today; therefore, they are constantly planting seeds. They are given the same 24 hours each day as everyone else, but they make sure that each day is lived to the fullest, most productive way possible. They understand that while others are watching their favorite television shows and having a good time at parties, clubs, social functions and bars, they must work on strategies, action plans, and timelines in order to bring them closer to their desired goal. This is not to say that they never take

time out to attend social functions or enjoy some form of entertainment, but they are modest in this area while they are striving to achieve a desired goal. Their days are mapped out and sufficient time is delegated for the achievement of their success. They sacrifice time that may otherwise be spent on a variety of luxuries and pleasures in order to have long-lasting luxuries and pleasures in the future. To be prudent and wise is to be able to use time well and when we use time well, we become less stressed about the concerns of tomorrow. To know the right use of the present moment is of extreme importance. Successful people know that.

The success-minded manage their money well.

Successfully wealthy people do not spend money frivolously. They know that when it comes to money, it is not about how much of it they make, but how much of it they save and/or invest that makes the difference. They recognize that money does play a big part in their success and therefore, they are savvy with their spending and strategic with their saving. When pursuing long-lasting success, they do not spend haphazardly or emotionally. Emotional spending occurs when people buy things they really do not need because they think it will make them feel better. Before doing this, the success-minded reflects on their goals and considers the cost of what it will be to accomplish those goals verses frivolously spending money on what they do not need. The success-minded also realize that if they do not have the money, but have the passion, the money will come.

Success-minded people realize that small purchases can make the difference between being a millionaire and being broke. The average person spends money as they wish. As soon as the money comes in, it goes right back out and oftentimes for things other than bills. When this happens, a cycle of living from paycheck to paycheck is perpetuated. There is no financial plan, no spending strategy, and no extra money available in case of emergencies. Managing money is an area that requires discipline, and the success-minded know that.

The success-minded manage their friendships.

Success-minded people understand that the company they keep will either enhance them or diminish them. Therefore, they make sure that they surround themselves with those who can make beneficial deposits into their lives. These deposits may be through a variety of ways, but they are all beneficial. For instance, they may have a friend who encourages them when they are having relationship issues, another who is there for spiritual uplifting, still another to give good, sound business advice, and yet another to hang out, shoot the breeze and let their hair down with. Everyone needs friends. Some have more than others because of their outgoing personalities. Others have only a few, but it is human nature to desire some form of companionship. It is also psychologically and emotionally healthy, but it is the quality of friends that will either hinder or help you. In chapter two, toxic relationships were discussed. With toxic people in your life, you cannot truly enjoy the success you are working so hard for. Therefore, it is of the utmost importance that your friends are an enhancement to you. Abundant living does not begin with goals only, but core values. Core values determine the quality of friends you have. Core values measure the levels of standards you live by, and sets the degrees of success you experience. Bad associations will corrupt a good character and the success-minded realize that.

The truly successful person embraces, practices, displays, and epitomizes integrity. Keep in mind that when I refer to success, I am not specifically talking about dollars and cents, although money comes to the truly successful as a byproduct. I am talking about wholesome success, the kind that comes from honesty and hard work; the kind that is begotten of sacrifice, toil, service and integrity. The distinction must be made because what the world perceives as success is not necessary success in the purest sense of the word. We tend to view people as successful because of their expensive and highly impressive material possessions, or their massive bank accounts, their influence over others, or the power they have in the world; if a person has acquired all those things, or have done so by dealing drugs, then is that real success? If they have betrayed and backstabbed others in order to advance monetarily, is that true success? If one has robbed, murdered and stolen to get where they are, then are they truly successful? True success comes with peace in the heart, contentment in the soul, and joy in the spirit. Therefore, truly successful people do not sacrifice their integrity in their pursuit for goal-achievement.

Webster's New World College Dictionary defines integrity as, 'The quality or state of being of sound moral principle, uprightness, honesty, and sincerity.' When most people hear the word integrity, they generally think of those same words, but integrity is not just being honest, but rather *why* people are honest. In other words, where does the conviction to be honest and to embrace virtues come from? Integrity is imbedded in internal truth, honor, and consistency. We are what we do, we are how we behave, we are what we think. When integrity drives our motives, we are less inclined to attach ourselves to those things that are dishonest, deceitful, and unscrupulous no matter how appealing the payoff may seem to be. When there is any element of deceit contained in a decision that is to be made, it behooves the person who is driven by integrity to withdraw themselves from such a temptation. As I close this chapter, I leave you with a quote from Author and Motivational Speaker Zig Ziglar as he spoke on integrity. *The foundation stones for a balanced success are honesty, character, integrity, faith, love and loyalty.*

Success Keys

- It is one thing to be born poor, but quite another to live poor and die poor. We may not all be born rich, but we may acquire riches through the creative use of our minds.

- Being elevated from good to great often requires risk-taking, which plays a big part of achieving your vision of success. Everyone at some point in their lives will take risks.

- Going from good to great means having an excellent work ethic. Being excellent is what stands you out among the rest and makes you unique.

- Making sacrifices is something that all successful people have done in order to get where they are.

- When integrity drives our motives, we are less inclined to attach ourselves to those things that are dishonest, deceitful, and unscrupulous no matter how appealing the payoff may seem to be.

8

Can you Handle Success?

In order to succeed, your desire for success should be greater than your fear of failure.

~Bill Cosby

Many people say they want to be successful, but not everyone can handle success. Not everyone is willing to put in the time, effort and sacrifice that it takes to be successful. However, there are those who have a dogged tenacity to succeed no matter what, and they are the ones who persevere in spite of the obsacles they face. They overcome setbacks, are self-discplined, confident that they will succeed and diligently plan their work and work their plan. They get the reward. The fruit from their seeds materiailzes and they reap the benefits from their sacrifices. The secret of a successful life is to be like a duck, smooth and unruffled on the top, but paddling furiously underneath! Reaping the benefits of your hard work and diligence is an exceedingly self-gratifying gift for the hard working success-pursuer. Nothing can match the feeling of experiencing the embodiment of what you have worked so hard for. Setting meaningful goals, creating action plans for your goals, then identifying realistic timelines requires a well thought-out plan, strategy, creativity, and focus. There is no comparison to that of having achieved success as a result of your own toil, labor, and work, but not everyone can handle success on a massive scale.

There are some who actually get there. As a result of following through on their goals and readjusting them when necessary, they do realize their dreams, but when they get there, they have no idea what to do. For them, a certain level of success is manageable, but when success has manifested in great avalanches, it can be difficult to handle and can even be overwhelming at times. If you had the expanded consciousness to conceive that level of succces, then you still have the expanded consciousness to handle that level of succces. The only way things come into fruition in our lives is when we have the mental capacity to receive them. Some people cannot receive things because mentally they cannot handle them. This is why you hear stories of people winning the lottery, and in two years they are flat broke. They did not have the mental capacity to handle their riches, so the riches left.

With success comes many open doors, great opportunites, new business ventures and a slew of new "friends". Success also brings influence, power, connections, and of course money; but it also brings temptations, pressures, false aquaintances and a new perspective about things, situations, and people. If not channeld properly, some of these elements can be a bit too much and may cause one to become stressed, drained and discouraged. Success draws both good and bad therefore, it is imperative that a life-balance is maintained in order to remain focused, grounded, and level-headed. The same self-discipline it takes to achieve goals is the same self-discpline it takes to remain at peace. In the beginning, the fruit of success will feel very good, but the feeling will wear off as you become accustomed to your new way of living; however, you are still expected to maintain that which you have achieved in order to remain where you are. Being able to do the things you were not able to do before by affording things you could not afford before, going places you never went before, and meeting people you probably would have never met before makes you feel important and influential, which is what the majority of people in this world want. I use the word majority, because not everyone wants massive success that allows the influx of those things. Some people simply want peace of mind, basic necessities, a simple, quiet life and to be left alone. They want no more and no less than what they have and nothing is wrong with that, but for you who think you want the whole shebang, you must be ready to accept the good, the bad and the ugly because it is not all good. The stress factor is a big element, especially for those who have achieved success to the degree that it has commanded attention and accolades. The commitment to maintain your success, to keep deadlines, and making the right daily decisions can produce what I call, "success stress." The only way to handle success stress is to get a handle on it before it gets too out-of-control. That is when self-discipline comes to play.

Good & Bad Stress

To be able to handle success is to be able to handle stress. From children to adults, everyone experiences stress on some level. Some have higher levels and some lower levels, but not all stress is bad. There is good stress and there is bad stress. How many celebrities have you heard of who have had nervous breakdowns from the pressures of being famous? How many have you heard of who committed suicide? How many began doing erratic and outlandish things (which is evidence of a breakdown)? They were not able to handle the pressures that came along with their massive success. The stress overtook them and for a time, they were no longer able to have clarity of thought. Being pulled in so many different directions can be taxing. Coping with stress is coping with new challenges effectively and properly handling the existing ones. Below and on the next few pages are some methods for dealing with success stress and keeping your levels under control. These methods will not eradicate stress, but they will certainly help to diminish it:

Time Management

Everyone is given 24 hours a day and seven days a week. What we do within each day determines what we will be doing in the days to follow. The improper use of time has caused stress to emerge in the lives of many. As a success leader, running out of time is one of the most challenging aspects we face, and not having enough time sometimes causes pressure, which causes stress. Driven people face this challenge almost daily. Why? Because they are always doing things. They stay busy, which is good because they are never idle. I once read a quote that said, *If you need something done, get a busy person to do it. The idle person has too many excuses and knows too many substitutes and short cuts.* Busy people get things done. Time is never on their side because they are always working on something new, something meaningful, something that will bring them benefits! It is important that you understand the difference between being busy and being productive. There are many people who stay busy, but their busyness is not bringing them any closer to the fulfillment of their goals. We all have errands to be done, which may include picking up clothes from the cleaners, buying groceries, cleaning the bedroom, getting the car washed, getting our hair done, etc. those are busy time-fillers, and yes, they are necessary, but you must spend an equal amount of time

> *As a success leader, running out of time is one of the most challenging aspects we face, and not having enough time sometimes causes pressure, which causes stress.*

working on your goals. This may include calling clients, updating your website, working on a chapter in the book you are writing, preparing a business proposal etc. These things may keep you busy, but at least you are productively busy. This is the difference between nonproductive busy and productive busy. Maintaining success will require effective time management and efficient productivity. When you find yourself engrossed in an inordinate amount of busyness, but feel that you are not being productive, then reorganize your time and readjust accordingly.

Another thing that may help with managing your time well is making a to-do list each day. I know it sounds simplistic, but it actually works if you stick to it. If you write down what you need to accomplish each day and commit yourself to everything on your list, you will be productive. An even further strategy is to knock out the most difficult thing on your list **first**. When you do this, you will find that the day seems smoother and stress levels are low. Taking care of the hardest thing first removes that level of stress that begins to rise from not taking care of it as yet, as the day slips by. This will also remove the temptation to procrastinate on it. When you find the day escaping you, readjust yourself and work on the things left on your list. This will keep you on task and you will not get so behind in your priorities, so long as your priorities are on your list.

Meditation

We talked extensively about meditation in chapter five, so I won't spend a whole lot of time on it here; however, I want you to realize that meditation does not necessarily have to do with any type of religious practice. Meditation is simply spending time alone in the silence and emptying your mind. It can be an invigorating experience to get away from the hustle and bustle of phone calls, emails, text messages and being pulled in different directions to absorb oneself in the silence. I would have never thought that going into a room alone without any distractions and just sitting in the silence could feel so good. From the onset it seems crazy, but successful people know the secret to strategic meditation. There are times when I'm meditating that I don't want to leave because the silence has taken me into a vision of who I am in the mental realm. I live my best life through meditation. It is a lifestyle that is formed through daily habits. You can never travel anywhere in this world that you have not first traveled in your mind. Most often, where the mind goes, the body will follow. I am at peace in the silence and after emptying my mind, my body relaxes. There are times that I have so much on my mind that relaxing at first is not possible. When that happens, I just sit there and allow my thoughts to be emptied. I think about this... I think about that... My mind goes here... It goes there... When it is completely emptied from all of the thoughts of the day, and other random things, it finally becomes silent. Then, I transition to a place where I enter into peace. Meditation is an absolute must for the busy bees who always tend to run out of time. Meditation keeps you sane and gives you the ability to handle situations without blowing your top. Meditation helps with patience and calmness, and that is something that not all the money in the world can pay for. It must be practiced and exercised.

Overcome Procrastination

Without argument, procrastination is definitely one habit that distinguishes the mediocre from the high-achiever. Everyone is inclined to procrastinate because seemingly, there is always tomorrow; but procrastination will put you behind, leave you behind, and make you regret not taking care of important matters when you should have. Essentially, procrastination is putting off for tomorrow what you can do today. People procrastinate when they feel that the task being delayed has more time to be completed; but when you procrastinate too much, you put yourself in a position that delays you from going forward. Success-minded individuals overcome this habit of procrastinating, realizing that they will get much farther if they do the things that need to be done today verses putting them off until tomorrow, then the next day, then the next. It's the flesh that loves comfort, and we generally do not like to be taken out of our comfort zone. When we force ourselves to take care of matters that we could put off for tomorrow, we eventually change the inclination of the flesh to give in to comfort and begin tackling challenges head on. If you break the habit of procrastination, you will see a big difference in your life.

Find Time for Pleasure

All work and no play makes Jack a very dull boy and makes Jill a very boring girl. Why work hard for success when you will not take the time to enjoy life. Most people strive for success because they want money and the ability to be able to do what they want, purchase what they want, and travel where they want; but if you are too engrossed in maintaining your success that you never take time for pleasure, then what is the point of acquiring success? Just as you were committed to your goals, you must be just as committed to maintain a balance which includes time for leisure and pleasure. Set a date to go on vacation, take the family to the movies, have game night or a Sunday dinner at the house where you are completely disconnected from work. Go to concerts, plays, and events. Your life must be balanced. A balanced life is a healthy life and a healthy balanced life is a happy life. You do not want to be imbalanced in any area of your life because when that happens, there is an overage or shortage somewhere. When you plan leisure time in your weekly schedule, you will find that you are less stressed and happier about life.

Sleep

Many successful people rarely get eight hours of sleep. They are usually up at the crack of dawn and get in the bed in the wee hours of the morning to sleep, then they are back up early to pull another long day. These are the worker bees. They make things happen and feel that sleep is overrated, but although people may feel that sleep is overrated, the fact remains that everyone needs it. There is no way that one can function effectively without an adequate amount of rest. After 48 hours of sleep deprivation, the thought process is distorted, the body becomes weak, and the speech becomes slow. Everyone's individual sleep needs vary. The average person is able to stay awake for 16 hours and sleep on eight. Some only need six hours and they are just fine. Regardless of how many hours are needed for you to function effectively, the bottom line is that everyone needs sleep.

Exercise

Let me give my disclaimer here. I am no fitness expert. In fact, I am probably one of the last people who should be talking to you about exercise since I've just recently jumped on this bandwagon; but I want to share the benefits of what I have gained with you. As with anything, if there is no pain, there is no gain. As we get older, our bodies begin to talk to us and the message it conveys is not always good. Our metabolism slows down, energy levels diminish, and the eyesight begins to dim. Although there are some things we cannot change, there are some things we can change, which will lead to a much healthier, happier, and more energetic lifestyle. Without your health, you can do absolutely nothing. You can be the richest person in the world, and with your money, you may buy the finest doctors in the world, but your money cannot buy you the God-given gift of health. Exercise and proper diet is essential to enjoying a healthy life. There is no way around it. It does not matter what your age, race, or gender is, exercise and proper diet can benefit all. I have identified below five benefits of exercise that if applied, will lead a relatively healthy person to a more fulfilling and energetic life.

Not having any type of physical activity makes the bones stiff and makes it harder to move around. Exercising regularly will improve the strength in your muscles and will make it easier and faster to get around. Regular physical activity also increases your endurance by transferring oxygen and nutrients to your tissues. Regular exercise also aids the cardiovascular system in working more efficiently. When both the heart and the lungs are functioning optimally, you have more energy, and can get more done without becoming tired.

Exercise Fact #1: Exercise reduces the risk of certain diseases

It is without question that regular exercise increases health and has proven to prevent or diminish many diseases in the body. Millions of Americans suffer from chronic illnesses that could have been prevented or reduced through regular physical activity. Sleep experts recommend that we do 20 to 30 minutes of physical activity three or more times a week combined with some type of muscle strengthening activity. Included in this regiment should also be some sort of stretching.

According to the President's Council on Fitness, Sports & Nutrition (2012), regular physical exercise reduces the risk of developing or dying from some of the leading causes of illness and deaths in the United States. For instance, regular exercise reduces and may even prevent premature death, heart disease, diabetes, and high blood pressure. It can also reduce the risk of developing colon cancer and feelings of depression and anxiety. Exercising also assists in building and maintaining healthy bones, muscles, and joints, helps older adults become stronger and better able to move about without falling, and promotes psychological well-being.

Exercise Fact #2: Regular Exercise can reduce and maintain weight.

The weight that we carry is determined by the number of calories we eat each day minus what our bodies use. *Everything* we eat contains calories, and everything we do uses calories, including sleeping, breathing, and digesting food. Any physical activity, along with what we normally do will burn extra calories that would otherwise be stored as fat. Exercising also increases the metabolism and lowers insulin levels. The key to successful weight loss and improved overall health is making physical activity a daily part of your routine.

Exercise Fact #3: Exercise is a great stress-reliever!

Exercise increases the endorphins in the body, which calms you down, makes you feel good, and in turn reduces stress. Endorphins can be referred to as the body's natural pain relievers because they reduce pain. Some refer to endorphins as the brain's feel-good neurotransmitters because of what they do in the body. Exercise reduces stress because it is actually meditation in motion.

While exercising, you are focusing upon what you are doing at the moment, and tend to forget about the problems and challenges of life. With regular exercise, you are constantly shedding tensions through your movements and eradicating many unwanted elements that cause stress. The resulting energy and optimism that comes from exercise can help you to remain calm and clear-minded in your day-to-day activities.

Exercise Fact #4: Exercise increases your energy level

Increased energy levels are the immediate benefits of exercising. It may seem weird to say that exercising increases energy when a person may not have the energy to start exercising in the first place; but studies have proven that regular physical activity via exercise does increase energy levels. As your heartbeat increases with a good workout, more blood surges through your brain, more oxygen is absorbed by your cells, and you become more mentally alert and lucid. Another benefit of regular exercise is the fact that as you become stronger through it, so does your immune system. Exercise boosts immunity, which helps prevent illness, or at least reduces its length and intensity.

Exercise Fact #5: Regular Exercise Strengthens the Heart.

Exercise strengthens the most important muscle in your body - your heart. Just as you must exercise every other muscle in your body, it is the same with the heart. If not strengthened, it will become weak; and the way to strengthen your heart is by doing cardio exercises. When the heart becomes stronger, it pumps more blood into your body. When you are sleeping, your heart slows down. The American Heart Association recommends that individuals perform moderately-intense exercise for at least 30 minutes three days a week minimally.

    As you can see, physical activities have many benefits and helps to relax and clear the mind. Clearing the mind allows for a fresh approach to perplexing and stressful problems. In order to benefit from exercise, it must be regular, and part of a daily routine. The bottom line is that exercise increases your overall health and sense of well-being. Without a doubt, this will definitely help to reduce your stress. In addition to what has been described as ways to handle and maintain success, there are also other areas for which to watch out. If one is not careful, self-importance will begin to embrace the new mindset, which will bring on a superiority complex accessorized in pride, arrogance, and conceit. Humility should therefore be deliberately sought, embraced, and practiced. This will keep you down-to-earth, grounded, and unassuming. Not everyone wants to be humble. Some deliberately strive to be abrasive, superior, prideful, arrogant and conceited, because it feeds their power and boosts their ego in a distorted and convoluted way. Unfortunately, because of their "success" and money, they usually get away with behaving in such a manner because those they mistreat rely upon them as their source of sustenance in some way. This may be in the form of a paycheck, a position, a connection, a partnership or a provider. To use intimidation and harshness as a way to gain respect is not true respect, nor is it true success. Respect is not given. It is earned. True success is not conceit. It is humility. A man wrapped up in himself makes a very small package.

    Many say that money and success will not change them, but when success brings with it a great deal of money as a byproduct, it will, in some degree change them, and in all honesty, it should. You should not do the same things you use to do, nor think the same way you use to think. Doing the same things will get you the same results. With new success, new money, new friends, and new opportunities should come a new way of thinking - a better way of thinking, not a narcissistic or superior way of thinking. This is to say that you should be more vigilant about money, things, situations and people. Good decision-making is needed and necessary when you have entered into the world of the truly successful. Handling success is not hard, it just requires vigilance, acumen, focus, self-discipline, and balance. Don't sweat the small stuff, unless you are sweating it out on the treadmill. Be deliberate in what you do. Nothing is great and nothing is small. It is all a matter of perception. Be careful what you ask for because if you have asked for success by faith and have worked on achieving it by action, you will get it according to your faith and action. You are deserving of every good thing you ask for and work hard for. Just be wise in your dealings.

Accountability

Being able to handle success also means being accountable to others. Regardless of where you are in life, you are already accountable to someone to a certain degree. You are accountable to your supervisor on your job for your work performance. If you are married, you are accountable to your spouse. If you are a parent, you are accountable to your children. If you are an employer, you are accountable to your subordinates and/or the board of directors for the stability of the company/organization. If you are a student, you are accountable to your professors, etc. We are all accountable to others in some way or another; but in addition to the obvious accountability connections, you should also have a personal accountability partner. I always say that no one is an island. You cannot achieve anything meaningful solely by yourself. You need people along the way to help propel you to where you want or need to be. For those who know me or have read any of my other books, you know that I continuously talk about masterminding. This concept means to connect with other individuals with like minds and like spirits, then form an accountability alliance called your Mastermind Group. The group meets on a designated day and time each week, two weeks, or monthly. The purpose of the Mastermind Group is to be accountable to each other for the goals that each member has set. Members in the Mastermind Group develop yearly goals and action plans for themselves. Sometimes goals are set for five and ten years down the line. There are also goals and objectives for the Mastermind Group as a whole. Meetings are held on a frequent and consistent basis, and in the meetings, individual reports are read on the progress of goals that members in the group have made.

    A report is given from each person in various categories. The areas can also be modified to fit the type of mastermind group you have. The most common areas are spiritual, financial, educational, family, recreational, personal, health, business/career, and civic. It is vital that everyone in the group is in harmony with one another because dreams and personal goals are divulged, plans for accomplishing them are delineated, and guidance from members in the group is sought and given in the meetings. Aspirations are discussed in detail and direction and advice is given by members in the group. The Mastermind Meetings must be productive, beneficial, encouraging, inspiring, and serious in nature. When the student is ready, the teacher will appear. If you feel that you are ready to participate in a mastermind group, then find one that you fit well into and join it. If you cannot find one, then create one! The accountability component of being in a Mastermind Group is the piece that is essential because when you are held responsible for carrying out the things you say you are going to do, you are more inclined to get those things done. In an effective Mastermind Group, everyone benefits from the knowledge, education, and experience of everyone else. The mastermind principle holds the secret to power. This mastermind principle is exercised by people who surround themselves with other people with great minds. No one person has sufficient experience, education, and knowledge to make it in this world without the cooperation of other people. A group of minds allied together in a spirit of harmony will provide more thought energy than a single brain alone. The best way to show the world what you are going to do is by showing the world what you have already done. You must illustrate. Talk is cheap. You must demonstrate. You only accomplish as much as you can prove by manifestation. The credibility of your word is in your accomplishments. To be successful is to be able to handle your success. In light of what you have read in this chapter, the hypothetical question remains: Can you handle success?

Success Keys

* The only way things come into fruition in our lives is when we have the mental capacity to receive them.

* Success draws both good and bad, therefore, it is imperative that a life-balance is maintained in order to remain focused, grounded, and level-headed.

* Coping with success-stress is coping with new challenges effectively and properly handling the existing ones.

* Busy people get things done. Time is never on their side because they are always working on something new; something meaningful; something that will bring them benefits!

* Respect is not given. It is earned. True success is not conceit. It is humility.

9
Giving Back

Without community service, we would not have a strong quality of life. It's important to the person who serves as well as the recipient. It's the way in which we ourselves grow and develop.
~Dorothy Height

When your goals have been achieved through the strategic use of applied principles, and you have accomplished things that have brought in a harvest of goodness, a sense of self-gratification emerges inside you as you reap the benefits of your hard work and toil. As you continue to enjoy the benefits of your success, the time will come when you must go back and give back. Everyone's life should contribute something positive to this world in order to make it a better place. The world must continue to be forward moving and that can only be done when we, as inhabitants of the earth, keep it moving forward through the use of our minds and the manifestations of the ideas that are birthed in our minds. We were not sent to this earth to sit idly by and do nothing but eat, sleep, grow old, then die. We were sent here to contribute, to serve, and to enhance the world. Everyone has a divinely assigned task, and that specific task is an important piece to the big puzzle called the universe. Others should benefit from your assigned task in some way. Can you imagine the world without computers today? Out of the invention of

> *As you continue to enjoy the benefits of your success, the time will come when you must go back and give back.*

computers emerged many other inventions, such as word-processing programs and a litany of other software programs that are too many to count. The invention of email was one of the most widespread inventions that emerged from the invention of computers. Can you imagine life without email? The Worldwide Web, also known as the internet, was created by two cofounders, Vint Cerf and Bob Kahn. In 1991, the Worldwide Web opened up to the public by these two men, who are referred to as, 'The Fathers of the Internet'. Can you imagine a world without the internet today? Someone invented those things that mankind is now benefiting from. The use of their minds served to make the world better. Someone's mind conceived the computer, the internet, and email. Those people came to this earth and made an invaluable contribution. What if Vint Cerf and Bob Kahn sat on their gifts and never cultivated their ideas? Other luxuries that we enjoy today were conceived, cultivated, nurtured, and brought out of the mind into the natural realm by some human being who lived or are still living on this earth. Telephones, cell phones, DVD players, IPods, televisions, automobiles, airplanes, trains, penicillin, etc., were all ideas created in the minds of people living on this earth. Those people made their contributions. I remember a time when only rich people had cellular phones and they were extremely expensive. Now, everyone has a cellular phone, including children in kindergarten. Can you imagine life without cell phones today? What about ultrasounds? There was a time when women had to wait until they gave birth to find out what the gender of their baby was, but with the creation of the ultrasound and sonogram, expectant mothers no longer have to wait. Someone contributed to the world with these inventions. So, I remind you again, we were sent to this world to contribute, to serve mankind and to make this world a better place. How are you giving back?

No one has made it in this world without the help of other people. Never make the unintelligent mistake of saying, *I don't need anybody.* We all need someone. If you did not need anyone, then who would pick up your garbage when you put it out on the street? You need the garbage man to do that. Who would ring up your food items in the grocery store? You need the cashier to do it. Who would bring you your mail? You need the mailman to do it. Who would clean your teeth? You need the dentist to do it. Who would educate your children? You need teachers to do it. Who would manage your money? You need an accountant or a bank to do it. This world can only move forward with people helping each other. Someone helped you get where you are, and if you are not yet where you want to be, someone will help propel you there. For this reason, it behooves you to do the same for others. The most important single ingredient in the success formula is knowing how to get along with people. If there is no deposit, there will be no return. In every relationship, your attitude towards other people will determine how they respond to you. You will not be respected if you do not respect. Hard work will earn you success, but being kind to people will earn you favor. Since we all need each other, why not make it easier for people to help you by being kind to others?

When you realize that the implementation of specific success principles has worked for you, and you have found the keys that lead to your success, you must share what you have learned by teaching those success keys to others. Your success, your time, your talent, your skills and your treasures are not just for you to hoard and keep to yourself. When you refuse to share what you know or at least some of what you know, you are operating in a competitive spirit. When you are blessed with knowledge, gifts, resources, influence, money and/or material possessions, they are to be shared and used to serve. You will never keep anything long if you hoard them. The universe operates on circulation: an in-flow and an out-going. In order to continuously receive, you must continuously give. There is room for everyone's success. You do not have to compete. Many people climb the ladder of success, and reach the top, but forget to leave the ladder behind for others to climb. This is not a way to maintain your success. Not being willing to help others reveals an insecurity or fear inside you, which will ultimately become your downfall. Selfishness can be your nemesis without you realizing it until it is too late. Confidence, diligent work, vigilance, self-discipline, and generosity is a way to maintain your success; so in light of this, the successful must think of ways to share their time, talents, and treasures with those who may be seeking to achieve what they have already achieved. Below are some ways of giving back to the community, society, and the world by blessing them with your knowledge:

Volunteering

It was previously stated that time never seems to be on the side of the successful person because they are always working on something new and meaningful; but just as you find the time to do the things you want to do, you must find the time to volunteer and give of yourself. Capacity is a state of mind. You can do just as much as you believe you can do. Therefore, if you really want to take the time to volunteer, you can. Many organizations would lovingly welcome you. Depending upon where your heart is, you can volunteer your time at a place that is connected to your heart. In other words, you may have a soft heart for the elderly, for children, or for the homeless. Considering this, you may volunteer at the nursing homes, orphanages, or homeless shelters. Needless-to-say, there are thousands of places that need you. Some of the things you can do include, but are not limited to: tutoring children, reading to children at public libraries, sharing your success with young adults who are transitioning into their chosen career, being a career-day speaker at a school, speaking at workshops and/or seminars in your field, serving as a mentor to a child needing a positive role model, etc. Giving your time in this manner does not require a whole lot, only a few hours out of the month, but the little you give, blesses and impacts the receiver and is also food for your soul.

Start a Charitable Organization

A 501c3 is an organization where no one within the entity shares in profits or losses. 501c3s are often referred to as charitable organizations, and their goal is to benefit and serve the public, not to earn a profit. These types of organizations are tax exempt and many receive tax-deductible contributions under the Federal Internal Revenue Code. Some common examples of 501c3 organizations (or charities) include those such as the Red Cross, United Way, Salvation Army, Feed the Children, American Cancer Society, YMCA, Goodwill, Girls & Boys Clubs, etc. In order to start a charitable organization, it must be for religious, educational, scientific, literary, testing for public safety, athletic competition, or preventing cruelty to children or animals. Charitable purposes are defined as activities beneficial to public interest and serving an open class of people, not a limited number of identified people. In other words, you cannot start a 501c3 for Hispanics only, African Americans only, Chinese only, etc. The charity must benefit all and discriminate against none.

The main difference between a 501c3 and a business is that the business' goal is to make a profit and taxes are paid on the money made. However, a nonprofit organization's goal is to focus on the "greater good" through serving the community, society, and the world, not necessarily to make money, although money is needed to operate the charitable organization. When donations and grants are received, the 501c3 charitable organization cannot use those funds for anything unrelated to the company's mission. Charitable organizations receive grants from individuals, the government, and private foundations in order to operate, run effectively, and carry out the organization's vision. Another major difference between a for-profit and a non-profit is when a for-profit organization goes out of business. The assets left can be liquidated and the proceeds distributed to the owners or shareholders. When a nonprofit goes out of business, its remaining assets must be given to another nonprofit organization. Some nonprofits have become extremely successful and have greatly benefited the community and society for which it was designed to help. Starting a nonprofit is a great way to give back, but if you already are engaged in a business that has contributed to your success, then time would be a challenge for you. Starting a charity can be done, but choosing the right people to run it is key.

Start a Foundation

Starting a foundation is another way to give back. Foundations do almost the same things that charitable organizations do, but there are distinct differences. Foundations are organized by a family, individual, or corporation. They make donations by way of grants to other nonprofit organizations. Charitable organizations generally derive their financial support from grants, individuals, the government, and/or private foundations, but private foundations typically derive their funds from a single source, such as an individual, family, or corporation. Private foundations do not solicit funds from the public, but they make grants to other nonprofit organizations. Due to their private nature, the laws governing private foundations are more stringent, including a requirement that they give away at least five percent of their assets each year. This is how wealthy philanthropists give back to the community. You don't necessarily have to be super rich to do this, but generally foundations are started by families with lots of money.

Start a Scholarship Fund

One of the ways you can certainly give back is to start a scholarship fund in your name, your family's name or the name of someone whose memory you want to keep alive. You may even name if after your organization. There are many students who desire to go to college and have the intellectual wherewithal to succeed, but do not have the funds for college. Financial aid helps, but only so much. A scholarship from an outside source may help to ease some of the financial burden. If the scholarship does not pay for the entire tuition or first semester, it can most certainly help with books, a laptop, fees, meal plan, or something else. Not only does giving a scholarship in your name establish your legacy, but it helps a deserving college student, which is the goal. However, writing a check for a scholarship is one thing, but being involved is another. While giving back, you want to be present, active, and visible. Many philanthropists give back monetarily in different ways to different organizations, but they are not or cannot be visibly present, and understandably so at times. Certainly, if one has the financial resources to assist various individuals, charities, and or organizations, they cannot always be there in person, but their donation is always accepted and appreciated. Successful people are *always* busy and must manage their time well; however, if you can write a check and be there for the ceremony or presentation of the check, it has a much greater impact on the gravity of your gift.

Partner with a School, Organization, or Charity

This is another way to give back. Becoming a "partner" should not just entail the giving of funds, but should also include the giving of your time and talents. If you truly want to do something, you will find the time to do it. You could designate an entire day for career day at the local school to speak to classes about your occupation. You could set aside some time to get in the serving line and feed the hungry one day out of the month. You could find out where the local back-to-school drive in your neighborhood is and not only donate bookbags and/or schools supplies, but also help to distribute them. Your partnership with any entity should be a viable and active one, not just the writing of a check in order to feel that you are fulfilling your community service obligation. Yes, I do understand that being visible is not always feasible for the successful businessperson, but when you can find the time, it will be well worth it and is good food for the soul.

When I worked as an Assistant Principal, the school district implemented a program called, 'Principal for a day'. This was a day when schools were asked to choose a community leader as their 'Principal for a Day'. Leaders were asked to give up a day of their time and spend in the school as the principal. The community leader sat in the principal's office, delivered the morning announcements, visited the classrooms, talked to students, and essentially experienced what it was like to be the principal. I was in charge of the program at my school, so I was strategic and methodical in my choosing. The first year, I chose a local community figure. At the time, he was a police chief, the pastor of a church, and a talk show host on one of the top radio stations in the city. My goal in asking him to serve as principal for a day was to build a partnership between him and the school and possibly get some free advertisement on the radio. I took him to lunch afterwards and maintained my connection to him throughout the years. Whatever the school needed after that, he was there.

The next year, I was also strategic in who I selected. I chose a popular television news anchor. Not only did she come and serve as the Principal for a Day, but she brought her news team with her! Needless-to-say, our school was on the news that evening and again, I maintained the connection to her throughout the years. Each year, I chose someone who could benefit our school and our students in some way. They wanted to give back and we welcomed their partnership with us.

Mentoring

This is a common and excellent way to give back and if your protégé is with you throughout the day, it is convenient for you. Mentoring is a way of pulling someone behind you up and showing them the ropes. Through mentoring, you impart your wisdom and "some of" your success secrets into your protégé. It is not wise to divulge all that you know, but it is commendable to share enough that will help propel another person onward and upward as they benefit from your guidance and wisdom. When choosing a protégé, you must ensure that they are the right fit. Make certain that they are receptive to you and are appreciative for the things to which they will exposed to. If they are the right fit, they will appreciate you guiding them, teaching them, instilling in them, and exposing them. Mentoring does not always have to be in the form of business. It may also have to do with life in general, relationships, and/or the implementation of success principles in general.

In addition to mentoring others, you also need your own mentor. We are never too old to learn anything. No one is self-sufficient. It does not matter how positive, inspiring, or motivating you are, there will come a time when you need someone to inspire and motivate you. Life is designed for us to need each other. The preacher needs a preacher, the doctor needs a doctor, the teacher needs someone to teach them, and if a lawyer finds himself in trouble, he too will need a lawyer. The motivator needs a motivator; and let us not forget that the judge has One who will ultimately judge him. It is a valuable asset when there is someone who can fill the position that we need in our lives, but when the student is ready, the teacher will appear, and not a minute before. The student must be ready. Successful people should always have someone who follows in their footsteps in the form of a protégée, but it would behoove them to also have someone to which they can look up to and learn from. No one has such a reservoir of knowledge that they do not need to be taught anything anymore. The bottom line is that you should have someone behind you that you are pulling up and guiding, but also someone ahead of you that you can look up to and benefit from.

Join Organizations in your field

Although joining organizations in your field benefits you, it can also benefit others. Attending conferences given by organizations of which you are a member, keeps you abreast of the latest improvements, innovations, and trends in your field.

Additionally, it allows you to network with others with whom you can forge long-lasting business and personal relationships. By being an active member in some of these organizations, you may request to speak, give workshops, trainings or professional development in your area, hence giving back. Of course, when you are paid to speak or conduct seminars and workshops, then that is not considered giving back. Service is a gift, meaning you give it with nothing expected in return. When a gift is paid for, it ceases to be a gift; hence, it ceases to become service. The aforementioned short list of ways to give back is but a seed planted just to keep in the forefront of your mind that giving back is our obligation once we have attained some level of security and accomplishment that can be referred to as success.

Fundamentally, giving back is a way to plant seeds that will sprout a good harvest. It is an opportunity to do something good for someone other than yourself. A little bit of your time could mean the world to someone else, and the sacrifice of time you spend feels good to you at the end of the day. The fulfillment and joy that emerges from helping others are important reasons alone to volunteer. When you commit your time and effort to an organization or a cause that you feel strongly about, your soul is refreshed and your heart is expanded. If you are not involved in any charitable organizations or causes, then there is no better time than the present to do so!

Success Keys

* Everyone's life should contribute something positive to this world in order to make it a better place.

* When you refuse to share what you know or at least some of what you know, you are operating in a competitive spirit.

* When choosing a mentee or protégé, you must ensure that they are the right fit. Make certain that they are receptive to you and are appreciative for the things to which they will be exposed to.

* Successful people are *always* busy and must manage their time well.

* Fundamentally, giving back is a way to plant seeds that will sprout a good harvest. It is an opportunity to do something good for someone other than yourself.

About the Author

 Dr. Mia Y. Merritt was born and raised in Miami Florida and matriculated in the Miami-Dade County Public School System. She is an educator with over 19 years experience working as a teacher, Assistant Principal, College Professor and mentor. She is a Certified Keynote Speaker, Teen/Youth Facilitator, Prosperity Coach and Author.

Dr. Merritt has provided workshops, seminars and keynote speeches around the country to organizations such as the U.S. Department of Homeland Security, The Miami-Dade County City Mangers, FIU Executive Staff, University of Miami Public Relations Department, Family Christian Association and many more.

She is also a Minister of the Gospel and is the recipient of the 2011 African American Achiever's Award sponsored by JM Family Enterprises. Dr. Merritt was also selected by Legacy Magazine as one of South Florida's 25 Most Influential & Prominent Black Women in Business and Leadership for 2013. She holds a Bachelors Degree in Elementary Education, a Masters Degree in Exceptional Education, a Specialist Degree in Educational Leadership and a Doctorate Degree in Organizational Leadership.

Dr. Merritt is a published author of 15 books on the subjects of spirituality, personal development, prosperity, self-empowerment, and adult education. Her books focus on living in peace with oneself and others by making right choices and understanding cause and effect. He books focus on living with integrity and serving others. Dr. Merritt's challenges and experiences in life have produced in her the resilience, character and strength to persevere in spite of what challenges she face. She shares her experiences in order to inspire, encourage and remind that your past does not dictate your future.

Discussion Questions for Book Clubs

1. In what ways does having a positive attitude towards people help to contribute to success in life? Why does attitude matter?

2. On page two, it states, *"The secret of success is to do the common things uncommonly well."* Why does doing small, seemingly unimportant things well matter to your bigger goal of achieving success?

3. Why is knowing how to overcome obstacles important in your journey to noteworthy success?

4. Explain the difference between internal and external obstacles and why it is important to know the difference.

5. Explain self-initiative, self-awareness, self-respect, self-reliance, self-efficacy, self-esteem, self-gratification and self-actualization, and how each of these are necessary to your pursuit of success. Explain self-doubt and self-hatred and how these can sabotage your success efforts.

6. How can using the S.M.A.R.T. method for developing your goals ensure that your goals are really goals and not just things-to-do?

7. Most people equate money with success, but explain some valuable things that money cannot buy. Also explain how a person can be successful without having lots of money.

8. How can not being healed from past hurts make success seem unfulfilling?

9. Why is takings risks a necessary part of life? Explain an intelligent risk verses an unintelligent risk.

10. In what ways do you give back to others beside your family?

Books Written by Dr. Mia Y. Merritt

To order copies of Dr. Merritt's books and workbooks, please visit one of the following:

miaymerritt.com
www.amazon.com
www.barnesandnoble.com

Recommended Readings

- As a man Thinketh, James Allen
- Can you Stand to be Blessed, T.D. Jakes
- Developing the Leader Within you, John Maxwell
- From Good to Great, Jim Collins
- Invest in Yourself, Dr. Marthenia Dupree (aka The Chicken Lady)
- Prosperity is your Birthright, Dr. Mia Y. Merritt
- Releasing Emotional Baggage, Dr. Mia Y. Merritt
- Success, Glenn Bland
- Successful Women Think Differently, Valerie Burton
- The Greatest Salesman in the World Part I, Og Mandino
- The Greatest Salesman in the World Part II, Og Mandino
- The Laws of Thinking, Bishop E. Bernard Jordan
- The Mastery Key System, Charles Haanel
- The Power of Diligence, Selena Williams
- The Science of Getting Rich, Wallace Wattles
- The Seven Habits of Highly Successful People, Stephen R. Covey
- Think & Grow Rich, Napoleon Hill
- Turn Setbacks into Greenbacks, Willey Jolley
- Winning with People, John Maxell
- You Must Have a Dream, Ann McNeill

www.ingramcontent.com/pod-product-compliance
Lightning Source LLC
Chambersburg PA
CBHW070915160426
43193CB00011B/1466

Three Ugly Sisters